THE ENCOUNTER SERIES

1. *Virtue—Public and Private*
2. *Unsecular America*

Virtue –
Public and Private

Essays by

James H. Billington

Gilbert Meilaender

Robert E. Rodes, Jr.

Bernard Semmel

Edited and with a foreword by

Richard John Neuhaus

WILLIAM B. EERDMANS PUBLISHING CO.
GRAND RAPIDS, MICHIGAN

Published by Wm. B. Eerdmans Publishing Co. in cooperation with
The Rockford Institute Center on Religion & Society

Copyright © 1986 by Wm. B. Eerdmans Publishing Co.
255 Jefferson Ave. S.E., Grand Rapids, Mich. 49503

Library of Congress Cataloging-in-Publication Data

Virtue, public and private.

  (The Encounter series ; 1)
  Proceedings of a conference sponsored by the Rockford
Institute's Center on Religion & Society, held at the
University Club, New York City in June 1984.
  1. Virtue—Congresses. I. Billington, James H.
II. Neuhaus, Richard John. III. Center on Religion
& Society (New York, N.Y.) IV. Series.
BJ1521.V57 1985   291.5   86-4265
ISBN 0-8028-0201-X

Contents

Foreword   vii

James H. Billington
    Education and Culture:
    Beyond "Lifestyles"   1

Gilbert Meilaender
    Virtue in Contemporary
    Religious Thought   7

Robert E. Rodes, Jr.
    On Law and Virtue   30

Bernard Semmel
    Democracy, Virtue, and Religion:
    A Historical Perspective   43

Exploring Virtue:
A Report on a Conversation   53

Participants   82

Foreword

This small book is the product of a conference. There is nothing remarkable about that of course. But in my judgment and the judgment of the other participants, this happened to be a remarkable conference. In truth it did not just "happen to be" remarkable; its success is to be attributed to its participants, a group as distinguished as it is diverse. The "report on the conversation" included in this book reflects the intensity of the engagement of these men and women in a subject that should not and cannot ever be "settled."

To speak about virtue and the virtues is to touch upon almost everything we deem excellent in personal and public life. In the last few years "virtue talk" has experienced something of a revival. Some would say it has become fashionable to talk about virtue. If so, it would seem to indicate a dramatic cultural shift and reason for encouragement. Nevertheless, a subject should be judged not by whether it is fashionable but by whether it is important. And a conference should be judged by whether it contributes importantly to an important subject. I believe the essays and discussion in these pages meet that standard.

In a highly politicized culture such as ours, it is to be expected that some readers will want to know where this discussion fits on the political spectrum. The answer is that it does not. Some of the participants call themselves conservative or neoconservative, and other call themselves liberal or neoliberal. They include proponents of democratic socialism and proponents of democratic capitalism. There are pacifists among them and at least one or two participants who do not take umbrage at being described as cold warriors. I think it safe to say that all participants entertain a robust skepticism about all the politicized "thought slots" by which we are inclined to categorize and, too often, to dismiss other people's viewpoints. And it is manifestly true that all participants cherish the virtue of civility that alone makes possible the achievement of intelligent agreement—and intelligent disagreement.

The conference was sponsored by the Rockford Institute's Center on Religion & Society in New York City and was held at the University Club in June 1984. The Center is grateful to the Exxon Educational Foundation and its president, Robert Payton, for generously underwriting the costs of the conference. As director of the Center, I am greatly indebted to Peter Berger, our senior consultant, and to my colleagues John Howard and Allan Carlson of the Rockford Institute for their support and counsel. I am most especially grateful to assistant director Paul Stallsworth, who shepherded the conference from concept to catering in addition to drafting the report on the discussion. Cynthia Littlejohn brought her usual devotion and grace to this project, as she does to all the projects of the Center.

Richard John Neuhaus

THE ROCKFORD INSTITUTE
CENTER ON RELIGION & SOCIETY
NEW YORK, NEW YORK

Education and Culture: Beyond "Lifestyles"

James H. Billington

Americans do not generally understand the basic fact that we differ greatly in our inherited beliefs and traditions from most of the rest of the world. Much of our uniqueness is rooted in the difference between the American Revolution for liberty and later revolutions seeking either fraternity or equality (i.e., national revolutionary movements like that of the French in 1792-94 or social revolutionary movements like that of the Russians). However, Americans have particular difficulty recognizing the basic difference between our kind of political revolution to create a constitutional order and to limit central power and these other more characteristic modern forms of authoritarian and secular revolutionary movement.

The American system is different, then, from most of the world in its origins and early development, but it has absorbed some of these other ideals while moving from isolation to interdependence in this century. Created as the United States of America and never called a nation in its founding documents, we came increasingly to be called a nation in the nineteenth century, particularly during and after the Civil War. In the late nineteenth and early twentieth centuries we developed a kind of nationalist ideology that remains here, as elsewhere, the principal temptation of conservatives within our political system and sometimes seems in danger of decomposing into pure faith in material strength defined in statistics and expressed in weapons.

In the late nineteenth and early twentieth centuries, Americans also domesticated their own version of a socialist ideology, which has become the temptation of radical reformers on the left. Their passion for radical redistribution fueled by class conflict often puts them in league with organized forces for social revolution globally. This socialist temptation on the left, like the nationalist temptation on the right, has its own characteristic American form of decomposition—concurrently into a kind of intellectual and material disarmament in the name of universal ideals but to the unilateral benefit of totalitarian enemies.

Beyond these temptations on the right and left within our system is the more prevalent and more unrecognized temptation in the center, in our own dominant tradition of liberty. This is the temptation (unfortunately entertained at the highest levels of the American establishment, among conservatives and liberals alike) to decouple freedom from its Siamese twin of responsibility. This decomposes freedom into self-indulgence and suggests that moral and political problems can be resolved with engines of self-enrichment, mere material expansion, and economic manipulation. This materialistic perversion of the ideal of liberty, this freeing of freedom from responsibility, may represent the most immediate present peril to our civic health and perhaps even to our survival.

Where is freedom without responsibility better exemplified than among what might broadly be called the American elite today? Conservatives seek freedom from the government without accepting greater personal responsibility for things government has been asked to do. Liberals seek freedom from personal responsibility by transferring as many problems as possible back to impersonal bureaucracies.

As individuals and historically in our tradition, we have acknowledged that there is only one answer to the inevitable question of who it is that we are responsible to. "Great God, our King" are the last words to "My Country, 'Tis of Thee." This was a very different transcription of the original British anthem from that of, say, revolutionary Germany, which translated "God Save the King" into "Volk im Gewehr" (people, to arms!), which is closer to all the bloodier, later national anthems modeled on the Marseillaise.

But the simple fact is that while most Americans believe in God—many fervently—most of the rich, the educated, and the opinion-forming elite in our country do not. A recent survey of 140 randomly selected leaders in the television industry showed that while ninety-three percent of them had had a religious upbringing, exactly the same percentage seldom or never attended religious services. Few educational leaders are willing to proclaim a personal religious commitment publicly the way Nathan Pusey did at Harvard twenty years ago.

The problem is even more grave with what I would describe as the second historic belief of the American people, which is in many ways only an elaboration of the first: belief in an objective moral order to the universe. The elite increasingly tend to believe in a subjective aesthetic disorder of their own creation. Washington seems increasingly fascinated with the aesthetics of power and increasingly indifferent to the content of policy. The rich reassure themselves that they are morally superior to ordinary people by patronizing the arts, decorating their pleasure domes with the icons of an indulgent modernity, often creating (more out of spiritual boredom than reformist conviction) synthetic and transient trends in politics no less than in fashions.

If this replacement of moral by aesthetic criteria is the main threat to our civic culture, television is the main culprit. In a world of moving pictures, pulsating sounds, swinging people, and television-shortened attention spans, we may be creating a new generation of "vidiots." Television has unquestionably become the value former in our civilization and the most ubiquitous teacher that any civilization has ever had—running for an average of seven and a half hours a day in ninety-eight percent of American homes, exposing most Americans (as of five years ago) to more than 13,000 killings, 100,000 violent episodes, and half a million commercials before they are eighteen years old—all of the carnage and come-ons immersed in a flood of fast-moving, wise-guy dialogue.

Television corrodes involvement let alone commitment in the civic arena, fostering a passivity and spectatorism that destroys interest in issues and participation in their resolution. In this sense it threatens basic civic decencies and shared social goals among a pluralistic people.

Belief in God, in an objective moral order, and in a civic virtue has weakened far more among the American elite than among the public as a whole. Less articulate groups have now begun to speak up for the slighted traditional values. They have called for prayer and the teaching of "creationism" in schools and for more moralists and patriots on television and in public life. Almost the only public morality that is publicly and passionately proclaimed by the mainstream of the university-media complex is their moral indignation against these other people. But denying something that may itself sometimes be negative does not lead to anything positive and tends to demean rather than redeem. Must we simply be forced to choose between those who are intellectually but not morally demanding on the one hand and those who are morally but not intellectually exacting on the other?

A final area in which the values of the American elite are perhaps in even greater conflict with the values of the American people as a whole is a unit of authority that traditionally follows God and country—the family. I am referring not simply to high divorce rates and greater sexual permissiveness among the affluent and educated but to an increasing inability even to distinguish between the liberal virtue of tolerating diversity in social arrangements and sexual practices on the one hand and a perverse tendency to force the public culture to attribute equal value to all norms on the other. President Carter, a man of incontestable personal commitment to the traditional family as an institution, found himself in his public capacity sanctioning the multiplicity of models called for in the new morality when he agreed to rename his White House Conference on the Family a "Conference on *Families.*" In the universities to which the American elite generally confine their late-adolescent children, virginity has itself become a form of deviance from the norm of experimental cohabitation that is publicly unchallenged by any university authority figures—and perhaps least of all by the chaplains.

Nothing better illustrates the fact that moral standards have eroded and been replaced by amoral, aesthetic criteria than the dreadful new word invented by the elite to excuse it all: *lifestyle.* If life is just a matter of style, one is just as good as another; another is probably better; and one-after-another is best of all. Indeed, the word *lifestyle* has become almost inseparable from the modifier *alternate.* The problem is that there simply are not any proven alternatives to the traditional family. Quite apart from moral considerations, societies that endure have always been rooted in the family system of nurture.

Far from challenging (or even diagnosing) our deep cultural

crisis, our university leadership community has tended to become a leading (albeit unwitting) example of the basic problem of freedom without responsibility. This is, of course, the basic condition of the tenured faculty that controls these institutions—almost unlimited freedom, considerable power to shape the new elite, and almost no responsibility to transmit the heritage of the past or to educate their students as full human beings. The disappearance of these two historic functions of American higher education has gone almost entirely unnoticed even as the crisis has deepened. The shift in the academy during the last fifteen years from self-righteousness to self-pity, from ideology to methodology, does not represent moral (or even intellectual) progress so much as a retreat under economic pressure to a more secure line of defense against any real accountability to the broader world.

By failing to affirm the particular ideals they have inherited or the specific people (students) they serve, the university elite is failing even to promote the general ideal in which they do believe: the unlimited advancement of knowledge. Historically (and, I would argue, logically) people have come to pursue truth as a generalizable objective in society in places where a sense of human possibility and of divine purpose have both been present. Unlike the secular ideals of equality and fraternity, liberty does not entail benefits to some only at the expense of others. All can be free if more are responsible, but only if freedom is increasingly channeled into the life of the mind and spirit. There alone, in an age of increasing material scarcity, are discoveries potentially beneficial to all. The pursuit of truth is the highest expression of freedom and may be the only way to keep us ultimately from the pursuit of each other. Our mental and spiritual faculties lift us above the apes, just as our animal nature keeps us lower than the angels.

One of our obligations as a people may be to recognize that in a simpler world America was called to liberalize a conservative polity, a mature America in a troubled world may face the obligation to conserve the evolutionary liberal ideal against revolutionary new authoritarian challenges. The renewal of civic values may require social restrictions on television as well as some new forms of obligatory public service for the young. Military service, for instance, might serve democratically to reinvolve the elite in the responsibilities that are concommitant with freedom. But no obligatory service will be meaningful (and indeed, any such service could end up as service of a perverse neonationalist authoritarianism) unless we institute it in conjunction with a revival of the pluralist-voluntarist tradition of doing things from the bottom up rather than from the top down (as our university-trained elite prefers). Family, parish, and immediate needs (rather than impersonal organization, media imagery, and symbolic causes) are the essential building blocks for restoring responsibility in our civic culture. Local primary and secondary schools must exemplify this ideal as well as teach it.

In the area of universal primary and secondary education, the need is to combine a common civic education with a diversified but deep spiritual education. We have yet to begin devising either the curriculum for the former or the structures for the latter. Something unifying along the model of the old public schools' invisible values of the American experience should probably be combined with released time for religious instruction for all parts of our heritage (including the Buddhism of new Asian-Americans and the like, and whatever personal-philosophical ideas agnostic and other nonreligious groups may wish to impart). The balance between the shared and the special is delicate and is best resolved at the local level rather than the bureaucratic-centralized level.

In the area of higher, university education, the greatest needs (which can be satisfied without challenging the structure and procedures of modern research and the requisite standard-affirming aspects of the university system) are, first, for more role models and individuals in administrations and faculties willing to teach the whole person (this would involve new categories of teachers as well as some recognition of people's values, experiences, and so on in hiring) and, second, some institutional commitment to transmitting a "core" of their own tradition as part of what is required for a degree. A plurality of cores from different places would be expected—but as an expression of a responsible commitment to define one at each place that calls itself a university. The very act of defining what the minimal core of our heritage now is would be a healthy exercise for faculties, who generally come together these days to discuss procedure rather than substance.

Virtue in Contemporary Religious Thought

Gilbert Meilaender

What parents have always known, students of religious ethics have recently rediscovered: it is important to think about character, about virtues and vices. Whether those engaged in scholarly study of virtue are, like the average parent, interested in actually inculcating virtue may be difficult to say, but there is no denying the increased interest in recent years in a theory of the virtues. And so, for example, in his *Survey of Recent Christian Ethics*, Edward LeRoy Long, Jr., devotes three chapters to the topic of moral agency, discussing recent treatments of ethics from the agent's perspective and emphasizing such concepts as virtue, character, conscience, and moral development.

How are we to account for this rediscovery of a very ancient theme in ethical reflection? In part, this focus on virtue suggests a widespread dissatisfaction with an understanding of the moral life that emphasizes duties, obligations, troubling moral dilemmas, and borderline cases. Such cases are interesting and certainly important when they arise, but we must admit that many of us go through long stretches of life in which we do not have to decide whether to convict one innocent man in order to save five, whether to lie to the secret police in order to hide someone fleeing tyranny, whether to approve aborting the ninth, possibly retarded child of a woman whose husband has deserted her, and so forth. An ethic of virtue seeks to focus not only on such moments of great anxiety and uncertainty in life but also on the continuities, the habits of behavior that make us who we are. Not on whether we should convict one innocent man to save five but on the virtue of justice, with its steady, habitual determination to make space in life for the needs and claims of others. Not on whether to lie to the secret police but on that steady regard for others that leads us to use language truthfully and thereby makes possible a common life. Not on whether abortion is permissible in an extreme case but on the ancient question Socrates raised— whether it is better to suffer wrong than to do it.

Such an emphasis on the texture and continuities of the moral life may well attract us, but it is not without its problems. It may seem to focus too strongly on the subjective and the relative—on the self. Both the attractions and the dangers are evident in a statement such as the following from Edmund Pincoffs' article "Quandary Ethics":

> The general point I have made is that what would be right for anyone in the same circumstances . . . is not necessarily right for me. Because what I have to take into account as well as the situation is the question what is worthy of me: What may I permit myself to do or suffer in the light of the conception I have of my own so far formed, and still forming, moral character?[1]

That this may be dangerous is clear. An emphasis on the objective and universalizable features of moral obligation represents a drive for fairness and a concern to discipline the self-regarding impulses that in large measure shape our action. But even if we grant that some of our moral responsibilities constitute, to use Kant's language, "duties of perfect obligation" and that these help to discipline our tendency to view our own case as exceptional, it may still be true that there is considerable place in the moral life for the first-person singular.[2] To decide otherwise is to deprive us of the freedom to determine our way of life in such

---

1. Pincoffs, "Quandary Ethics," in *Revision: Changing Perspectives in Moral Philosophy,* ed. Stanley Hauerwas and Alasdair MacIntyre (Notre Dame, Ind.: University of Notre Dame Press, 1983), p. 101.

2. For a more detailed development of this argument, see my article "Is What Is Right for Me Right for All Persons Similarly Situated?" *The Journal of Religious Ethics* 8 (1980): 125-34.

a manner as to consider it peculiarly ours. It is, in the words of Stanley Hauerwas and David Burrell, to obligate us "to regard our life as would an observer."[3]

And it is morally important that we not regard our life as would an observer—important enough that we should run a few risks to emphasize it. Consider the following story, related by Leon Kass:

> A shabbily dressed elderly man has come to consult the professor of philosophy with a question about business ethics. "Me and my partner, we have a confectionary store in the Bronx. Last week in comes a young man, very distracted, probably in love, asks for a package of cigarettes. Staring dreamily at the ceiling, he puts down a $10 bill, takes his cigarettes and starts out of the store, leaving his change on the counter. Now, Professor, comes a question, business ethics. Should I or should I not tell my partner?[4]

The point of the story? The moral dilemmas we perceive depend upon the persons we are. Recognition depends upon character. What duties we perceive—and even what dilemmas—may depend upon what virtues shape our vision of the world.

To see this is to see an important reason why religious thinkers, in particular, may be drawn to the turn toward virtue in ethical theory. If action flows from vision and vision depends upon character, then religious beliefs may be of great importance in the shaping of an ethic. Religious disciplines (e.g., confession and prayer) may affect what we see and do by shaping the persons we are.[5] This suggests possibilities for breaking through—or bypassing—the seemingly endless debates about the relation of

---

3. Hauerwas and Burrell, "From System to Story: An Alternative Pattern for Rationality in Ethics," in *Knowledge, Value and Belief*, ed. H. Tristram Engelhardt and Daniel Callahan (New York: The Hastings Center, 1977), p. 127.

4. Kass, "Ethical Dilemmas in the Care of the Ill, Part I: What is the Physician's Service?" *Journal of the American Medical Association*, 17 October 1980, p. 1812.

5. On this, see Craig R. Dykstra, *Vision and Character: A Christian Educator's Alternative to Kohlberg* (New York: Paulist Press, 1981), especially chapters 2 and 4.

religion and morality that grow out of the Kantian tradition in ethics. The question will no longer be whether religion is somehow necessary to morality if morality is understood in terms of the vision by which we see the world, a vision shaped by our character, and a character shaped (for the believer) by the disciplines of the religious life. From the agent's perspective it is clear that religious belief will be involved in the shaping of character and moral vision. And of course the (re)turn to an ethic of virtue will also entail renewed consideration of the possibilities of vice, the need for sinners to be sanctified, and the importance of controlling and disciplining the unruly ego—all themes congenial to religious ethics.

We might imagine that the turn toward an ethic of virtue, if it is in part a turn away from an ethic shaped primarily by difficult and agonizing borderline cases, is a turn toward simplicity and away from complex, complicated ethical systems. In some ways, however, the opposite may be true. We cannot really talk very long about virtue without speaking of virtues—of particular moral excellences that go by various names. Indeed, enshrined in Western moral tradition at least from the time of Plato are the names of four cardinal virtues—prudence, justice, courage, and temperance. These form the hinge or axis (*cardo*) on which the moral life turns. To this tradition of four cardinal virtues Christian thought added the three theological virtues—faith, hope, and love. What we begin to have, then, is a complicated ethic capable of distinguishing many different traits of character and habits of behavior. Such an ethic speaks not only of obligation, or only of authenticity, or only of love. It is an ethic that permits more by way of moral evaluation than judgments of right and wrong. Our powers of moral evaluation would not be paralyzed just because in a given circumstance we could condemn a particular act as wrong. What we do not condemn as wrong we can still deplore as, for example, intemperate. An appreciation for nuance in moral evaluation should be a part of an ethic of virtue.

Finally, the renewed emphasis on virtue in the moral life involves, at least sometimes, an attempt to consider seriously the way in which communities shape character. "The idea of character involves not only qualities in the moral agent but also the communities to which the moral agent has been related and from which he draws norms, values and directions."[6] Character is shaped through moral education, and such education is carried on in communities, both small and large. Here too there are difficulties and dangers not always fully appreciated by those who develop an agent-centered ethic. For example, in his interesting and helpful study *The Use of the Bible in Christian Ethics*, Thomas Ogletree notes that, especially in the New Testament, "perfectionist" themes (that is, those having to do not with the goals or structure of action but with formation of the self) come to the fore, and such categories as "discipleship" become central for understanding the moral life. And he appears to reckon with the fact that the disciple's virtue can be developed only within communities distinctive enough to foster it. Thus he suggests that contemporary Christian ethics can best be done by those with (1) at least some degree of alienation from the institutions of the larger, surrounding society and (2) deep involvement with a distinctively different community. It turns out, though, that the distinctively different communities he has in mind are those that are egalitarian in thrust and that endorse and welcome cultural pluralism—in short, communities that endorse the prevailing themes of present-day academic communities. Indeed, Ogletree even suggests that "the gospel summons us to celebrate pluralism, to welcome it into the internal life of the community of faith."[7] A good suggestion, perhaps, but we may be permitted to wonder whether those pluralistic communities of faith that Ogletree celebrates will be any more successful at inculcating virtue and shaping character than the pluralistic society from which they are "alienated." In short, an agent-centered ethic raises social and political questions that it will be important for us to consider.

I

In *After Virtue: A Study in Moral Theory*, a book that must be judged remarkable even by those not persuaded by its thesis, Alasdair MacIntyre has suggested that we live in a disintegrating

---

6. Edward LeRoy Long, Jr., *Survey of Recent Christian Ethics* (New York: Oxford University Press, 1982), p. 198.
7. Ogletree, *The Use of the Bible in Christian Ethics* (Philadelphia: Fortress Press, 1983), p. 156.

culture made up of nothing more than fragments of earlier cultures. He contends that this fragmentation accounts for the moral chaos of our time. And yet his analysis is not entirely pessimistic. He suggests that we may have some reason for hope by comparing our own moment in history to that period in European history when the Roman Empire declined into the Dark Ages. "A crucial turning point in that earlier history occurred," he writes, "when men and women of good will turned aside from the task of shoring up the Roman *imperium* and ceased to identify the continuation of civility and moral community with the maintenance of *imperium*."[8] Instead, they tried to fashion new forms of common life, forms in which the virtues could be lived, sustained, and inculcated. MacIntyre's hope is that we may find ourselves at a similar moment. "What matters at this stage is the construction of local forms of community within which civility and the intellectual and moral life can be sustained through the new dark ages which are already upon us. . . . We are waiting not for a Godot, but for another—doubtless very different—St. Benedict."[9]

In fact, however, the beginning of the disintegration of the Roman *imperium* had begun considerably earlier, and long before St. Benedict there were others who thought seriously and rigorously about how to be virtuous in bad times, how to sustain character in diverse and disintegrating communities. In the last third of the second century after Christ, a great Roman emperor found himself in the northernmost portion of the Empire, doing battle along the Danube with barbarian invaders who were beginning to knock insistently at the door to Italy. Marcus Aurelius spent much of the last decade of his life and reign there, and, while battling the Quadi and Marcomanni, while administering from afar the affairs of the Empire, while suffering private sorrow and poor health, he penned his *Meditations*, one of the great documents of Stoic thought. Of the Stoics, and of Marcus Aurelius in particular, H. D. Sedgwick wrote,

> The ancient Stoics were in the same ignorance as seekers today who are no longer Christians. They had no authorita-

---

8. MacIntyre, *After Virtue: A Study in Moral Theory* (Notre Dame, Ind.: University of Notre Dame Press, 1981), p. 245.
9. MacIntyre, *After Virtue*, p. 245.

tive revelation, no word of God, to teach them the nature of the world in which they found themselves, no divine code of laws to tell them what to do. They looked about and beheld sorrow, disease, old age, maladjustments of all sorts, wars between states, civil strife, contention among neighbors, earthquakes, and tempests. Such was the world then; it is not very different now. In a world of this sort, what shall a man do to persuade himself that it is a world of order and not of chaos. That there is something in it other than vanity, that it has what the human heart, if the human heart had spiritual eyes, would pronounce to be a meaning? The Stoics were honest men and would not go beyond the evidence of the senses, they turned away from Plato's dream that the soul released from the body may behold divine beauty, and from Socrates' hope of communion with the heroic dead, and created what they called a philosophy, but what we may more properly call a religion, out of the world as their human senses saw it, a religion, austere and cold, but sane, high, and heroic.[10]

We should note that Stoic virtue was, at least in part, a response to changed political circumstances. The *polis* was gone; an age of empire had come, and political space was greatly expanded. Politics had become more a matter for bureaucratic administrators and less a matter of face to face encounter. In such a world a Stoic such as Marcus Aurelius certainly did not (to use MacIntyre's formulation) turn aside from "the task of shoring up the Roman *imperium*," but may nevertheless have executed an inner withdrawal.

For Marcus Aurelius, virtue becomes reverence for what nature gives, not persistent petition for what we desire. "Another [prays] thus: How shall I not lose my little son? Thou thus: How shall I not be afraid to lose him?"[11] "His reason," Sedgwick writes of Marcus Aurelius, "said that the universe is impersonal, and he turned from human desire, the human craving, for a Divine Friend, with a renunciation as ready as the welcome with which

---

10. Sedgwick, *Marcus Aurelius* (New Haven: Yale University Press, 1922), pp. 12ff.

11. Marcus Aurelius, *Meditations,* trans. George Long (South Bend: Regnery-Gateway, 1965), 9.40.

other men greet the great hopes of life."[12] Small wonder that
Matthew Arnold could call this emperor "perhaps the most beautiful figure in history."

I point here to Stoic virtue, against the background of
MacIntyre's call for new communities committed to sustaining
the virtuous life, in order to remind us of the powerful possibility
of inner withdrawal and the virtue that accompanies it. This
vision has been developed in a work by James Gustafson that is
in many ways more Stoic than Christian. If any figure in the
world of academic religious ethics can be said to have stimulated
the recent turn to an agent-centered ethic, it would be Gustafson.
His most recent work, *Ethics from a Theocentric Perspective*, is
a lengthy volume that draws together his views into a systematic
statement. The very title of the book suggests that his is a view
in which there can be no real separation of religion and morality.
And he notes on several occasions that any "ethic" that emerges
from his perspective may not seem much like ethics at all "in a
recognizable Western sense."[13] At any rate, it is clear that what
Gustafson offers is not a set of rules (he thinks the world too
complex for that), nor a full-fledged description of the virtues that
agents must have (he holds that to be impossible on the grounds
that the character must be continually transformed), nor a weigh-
ing of costs and benefits (since ethics cannot be a science). Instead, he offers an "ethic of discernment" in which "the final
discernment is an informed intuition" of a person moved by piety
for the divine governance of our world (p. 338).

One need only describe the tradition in which Gustafson
says he is writing to recognize that the focus of this ethic is always
upon the moral agent in relation, and especially in relation to
God. Gustafson takes pains to make clear that he writes from
within a kind of critical attachment to the Reformed tradition in
Christian thought. Calvin, Edwards, and H. Richard Niebuhr are
predecessors in that tradition who loom large in his understanding. The aspects of Reformed tradition that he particularly wishes

---

12. Sedgwick, *Marcus Aurelius,* p. 256.
13. Gustafson, *Theology and Ethics,* vol. 1 of *Ethics from a
Theocentric Perspective* (Chicago: University of Chicago Press, 1981),
pp. 81, 84, 99. Subsequent references to this work will be cited parenthetically in the text.

to appropriate are (1) the sense of a powerful, sovereign God who stands over against the creation; (2) an emphasis on the centrality for character of religious affections—dependence, respect, gratitude, obligation, and remorse; and (3) the imperative that we "relate ourselves and all things in a manner appropriate to their relations to God" (p. 327).

Gustafson not only appropriates insights from this tradition but also criticizes it. Chief among his criticisms, and one crucial for the kind of virtue that emerges, is a view to which he finds himself driven by the deliverances of modern science: he is unwilling to affirm that the sovereign governance of God orders events for the sake of human well-being. "It is precisely at this point that [my] argument . . . comes to its most critical problem with the Christian theological tradition. Barth says vividly and categorically: 'God is for man.' I do not say God is against man. But the sense in which God is for man must be spelled out in a carefully qualified way" (p. 181). It must, for example, be made clear that any hope for life after death is unnecessary in Christian theology (p. 184). Theology has, Gustafson believes, remained unfortunately "Ptolemaic" in its basic outlook (p. 109). It has taken as its central concern the welfare of human beings and has used God as a means to further our own desires. Gustafson is led to reject this tendency for two reasons. First, he contends that what we learn from science makes it "very difficult to sustain the belief that the cosmos was made for man" (p. 90). Second, he maintains that we should not value God for his usefulness to humanity. A Copernican revolution is needed; we must learn to construe the world from a truly theocentric perspective. Not faith but piety is the primary religious affection—piety understood as awe and respect for the divine governance, whether or not that governance is for our good. Religious affection, which molds and shapes character, is chiefly a piety in the face of those powers that bear down upon us and sustain us.

Indeed, the tendency of a more traditional Christian theology to see God as centrally concerned for the good of the human species is explained by Gustafson in terms of his metaphor for sin: contraction. We contract our sense of what is desirable to our own good rather than the health of the universe.

> One may properly ask why some larger, more dramatic, ultimate meaning and perfection is desired. What is so

attractive about the assurance given in the New Testament that all things will be made new? From the religious standpoint of this book, part of the explanation is that we do not consent to our finitude properly, that we do not consent to the place of the human species in the universe. (P. 310)

True piety will so consent, says Gustafson; it will avoid such contraction of the spirit.

It is in light of statements such as these that I described Gustafson's conception of virtue as more Stoic than Christian. The piety he endorses is not primarily a piety nourished by the Christian story. Nothing in particular makes Gustafson's view more *theocentric* than, say, Calvin's. The difference lies simply in the fact that the character of the *theos* Gustafson discerns is not definitively seen in Jesus' death and resurrection. This makes a decisive difference in his conception of a virtue like hope. What he perceives as an exaggerated hope may not be at all exaggerated for one whose piety is more decisively shaped by the second article of the Christian creed. From that more traditional perspective the true contraction of the spirit may be the unwillingness or inability to hope for all things made new.

Near the close of *Ethics from a Theocentric Perspective* Gustafson writes, "One of the themes of this book is that visions, ways of life, and intellectual activities take place in particular historical and communal contexts" (p. 317). But in fact—and those who know Gustafson's previous writing may be surprised by this—there is very little about communities in this book. Certainly the virtue of piety that Gustafson makes central and the vision of the world that both gives rise to such virtue and flows from it are unlikely to be developed in Christian communities nurtured by the story of Jesus. For that story is not, as Gustafson would have it, simply that "Jesus incarnates theocentric piety and fidelity" (p. 276); it is also a story that Tolkien (possessed perhaps of a keener literary sense) termed a "eucatastrophe," a story with a happy ending. And if we are actually to take seriously the particular historical and communal context in which Christian virtue is developed, we must reckon with that fact.

Gustafson's vision of virtue is not really, I suspect, the sort to be developed only in small communities by those who have turned aside from the task of shoring up modern-day empires and

have devoted themselves to sustaining the moral life through a
new dark age. The virtue he endorses is much more universal in
its potential appeal—the sort that would be interesting not only
to a Marcus Aurelius but also to an Epictetus. The withdrawal
it requires is internal. And if it seems at first too passive and
resigned to be effective in our world, we should remember that
detachment (the Stoic's "apathy") can be the first step toward
powerful and effective agency. But there is little in Gustafson's
discussion of the religious affections to suggest the necessity of
communities for shaping the moral life. To see the possibilities
in such an emphasis we must turn to another thinker, one who
has been shaped far more deeply by MacIntyre's vision of our
current predicament.

II

"The church does not have a social ethic; the church is a social
ethic."[14] With this statement Stanley Hauerwas summarizes what
has been a major theme in most of his writing. In an earlier work
he made the same point in a slightly more expanded formulation:
"The first task of Christian social ethics . . . is not to make the
'world' better or more just, but to help Christian people form
their community consistent with their conviction that the story
of Christ is a truthful account of our existence."[15] Hauerwas
contends, reasonably enough if we understand what he means,
that his is not an ethic of withdrawal; "rather it is a call for the
church to be a community which tries to develop the resources
to stand within the world witnessing to the peaceable kingdom"
(PK, 102). Still, it seems better to recognize that this is indeed a
withdrawal from the task of shoring up present political communities, even if the withdrawal is ultimately executed for the sake
of those communities. If the only hope for the world lies in the

---

14. Stanley Hauerwas, *The Peaceable Kingdom* (Notre Dame,
Ind.: University of Notre Dame Press, 1983), p. 102. Hereafter abbreviated *PK*. subsequent references to this work will be cited parenthetically
in the text.
    15. Hauerwas, *A Community of Character* (Notre Dame, Ind.:
University of Notre Dame Press, 1981), p. 10. Hereafter abbreviated
CC. Subsequent references to this work will be cited parenthetically in
the text.

presence within it of " 'cells' of people who manifest a joy that otherwise the world would have no means of knowing" (PK, 149), it is still true that Hauerwas's emphasis is on virtues inculcated within these smaller cells.

Withdrawal is, in part, forced upon the church by the surrounding culture. Hauerwas's criticism of our "liberal" society is rooted in his reading of political theory and in his theology. A liberal society, he argues, mistakenly assumes that a people can form a community without any shared story to bind their lives together (CC, 78). Such a society seeks no more than a shared system of rules to ensure fairness among individuals, for whom society is no more than an arena in which to pursue their interests. This system of rules, precisely in order to be fair, must be defensible in terms that are publicly acceptable and that any objective observer would share. Hence, it must exclude precisely those elements that make our histories personal and particular. Religious belief, from this perspective regarded as personal and private, must be excluded from the public realm in the name of fairness. Any moral views I hold must be justified in terms available to anyone. The first-person singular is excluded, and I am forced to regard my life as an observer would regard it. Individuality flourishes, to be sure, but only in private. In the public realm the individual's personal history—a vision of the good shaped by one's character and characteristic virtues—must be subordinated to a lowest-common-denominator set of rules that can be affirmed by all citizens, whatever their virtues or vices.

In another context we might well ask whether there is not more to be said for a liberal polity than Hauerwas seems to recognize, but here we will direct our attention only to what he does with this analysis. Clearly, he presents some valid criticisms of liberal societies. He recognizes rightly that if we bemoan the loss of "community" and attack "individualism," we may have to rethink the sort of public community we desire. It may not be a community that can be free and "open" about all matters. Loss of some freedom may be part of the price we must pay for community—that is, for a people whose lives are bound together by a common story. Some freedom may have to be sacrificed if we are serious about shaping character.

But now, another move: if we decline to shape character through the kinds of force available to political communities, and if a belief that the first-person singular is essential in morality prevents us from using the techniques of public argument to persuade those whose character has not been shaped by a shared vision, withdrawal to a smaller community in which consensus is still possible may seem both reasonable and necessary. Hence, the church must be more than just a community that shapes character; it must be a *nonviolent* community. The kingdom of God is a peaceable kingdom, says Hauerwas, in which the virtues of patience and hope are central (*PK*, 103).

I am not altogether certain that this reading of the direction of Hauerwas's thought is fair. Many themes interweave in his writing, and it is not easy to chart the paths by which he moves from one to the next. I have tended to make nonviolence a conclusion drawn from other themes; yet, in *The Peaceable Kingdom*, his most recent and systematic work, it plays a more pivotal role. He presents it quite simply as the way of Jesus and the way to which the disciple of Jesus is called. Nevertheless, the emphasis on character is the most enduring theme in Hauerwas's writing. Time and again he notes that the discipline of religious ethics has lost its moorings by concentrating on decisions and dilemmas rather than habits of behavior. Habits of behavior, our virtues and vices, shape the way we see the world, and in turn they are inculcated by the communities we inhabit and the stories that sustain those communities. This cannot occur, he maintains, in a liberal polity, where nothing is shared except a commitment to procedural fairness. Hence the need for withdrawal if we care about shaping Christian character but are unwilling to use forceful political means to fashion a community capable of producing such character.

This is the direction of movement I discern in Hauerwas's thought: withdrawal from a fragmented world in order that, for the sake of that world, virtue may be developed in the lives of some who will then present a living testimony to the world of alternative possibilities for human life. Clearly, the withdrawal required here is more than the inner individual detachment that Gustafson espouses. If it is withdrawal, it is far from detached or passive. If it is withdrawal, it remains political in character. It is the attempt on the part of communities of Christian people to understand themselves as separate and distinct—as wayfarers in the world, patient of that world because their hope is in God.

One example may help to clarify how this approach influences

Hauerwas's discussion of controverted moral questions. In a chapter of *A Community of Character* entitled "Abortion: Why the Arguments Fail," he argues that when Christians attempt to express their opposition to abortion in terms acceptable in our public debate, they necessarily set aside the most important reasons they find abortion so morally troubling. This is not entirely bad. Hauerwas notes that the achievement of liberal societies is precisely to remove from the arena of public debate those subjects about which people care most deeply (*CC*, 217). But abortion may prove to be one of those issues that cannot, in the jargon of our time, be "privatized."

What are the real roots of Christian opposition to abortion, the roots that cannot be uncovered in public debate? Hauerwas contends that Christians are called to be people of a certain sort—people who recognize God as Lord of life and death, people whose faithfulness to God is lived out in history and who therefore understand the presence of children as an expression of their intent to live within history as God's people, people who know themselves to have been loved by God even in their weakness and for that reason now seek to love the weak who cannot speak for themselves, people who understand the presence of children as a sign of God's continuing affirmation of his creation, people who believe that "God will not have this world 'bettered' by destroying life" (*CC*, 228). Christian concern about abortion cannot be understood by others except against the background of such beliefs—beliefs best expressed not in terms of entitlements or criteria of personhood but in terms of "the kind of people we ought to be to welcome children into the world," the sort of people who would be characterized by the virtue of hope (*CC*, 229).

The argument is powerful, in some ways compelling. I judge it to be one of the finest passages Hauerwas has written. And yet ... what are we to do with it? As Hauerwas himself clearly notes, these are not the sorts of arguments that seem acceptable in public debate about the common good of our political community. We are not permitted to rest much on the sort of character we think it wise to develop; public argument seems to turn on questions of rights and obligations. The political theorist Philip Abbott has noted how impoverished such public moral discourse can become: "Who would want to live in a society in which everyone was positively indecent to another and at the same time positively scrupulous in respecting another's rights?"[16] Hauerwas is expressing a similar concern, but it is a concern difficult to articulate in the terms of public debate within a liberal society. He grants that Christians may seek ways to work within the public arena, but the thrust of his argument is to suggest that the primary concern of Christians should be to shape communities of their own in which they learn to be people of a certain kind. This withdrawal will, in a sense, be for the world, since it is the only way the world may come to see what Christian conviction truly is. But it will be withdrawal all the same—a shift in focus from shoring up a decaying *imperium* to fashioning a community that in its very existence will be and live a social ethic.

III

Gustafson writes for individuals who must find virtues powerful enough to sustain themselves in an alien world. Hauerwas writes for the Christian community determined to shape character and forced by that determination to understand itself as a community set apart from the surrounding culture. In a recent book on medical ethics, William F. May writes for healing professionals who are driven into the world by the vocation but who find the resources of the culture inadequate to sustain their vocational commitment.[17] May finds much to criticize about the practice of medicine in our society, but, unlike Hauerwas, he does not seem to believe that character can only be developed in smaller cells alienated from the larger society. Indeed, he also finds much to affirm in the practice of medicine, and he suggests that what is good there can best be sustained when placed within a religious context. Unlike Gustafson, he does not urge us to develop the virtues needed to come to terms with a world indifferent to our fate; rather, he argues that "preoccupation with death and destructive power has replaced attentiveness before a good and nurturant God as the central religious experience of modern

---

16. Abbott, "Philosophers and the Abortion Question," *Political Theory* 6 (August 1978): 327.

17. May, *The Physician's Covenant: Images of the Healer in Medical Ethics* (Philadelphia: The Westminster Press, 1983). Subsequent references to this work will be cited parenthetically in the text.

people" (p. 32)—and this is bad! Gustafson argues that the ultimate powers in our world are, if not destructive, at least indifferent.
May agrees that many have come to believe this, but he does not
recommend that we develop the virtues of inner withdrawal that
will enable us to live in such a world. Instead, he suggests that
it is precisely our modern reverence for destructive powers that
has distorted the practice of medicine. We have come to assume
"that death defines, without significant remainder, the healer's
task" (p. 35).

The virtues we need are those that grow out of belief in a
creative and nurturant ultimate power, and the importance of
these virtues for medical professionals can be made intelligible
by appeal to the needs of the profession itself. May's approach,
then, is quite different from that of either Gustafson or Hauerwas. Like Hauerwas, he does his ethical reflection from a distinctively Christian stance, but he thinks he can show the intelligibility
and importance of Christian conviction for the healing art even
to those who have not been shaped by intentional Christian
communities. Like Gustafson, he emphasizes the role of vision
in the moral life, but he understands the task of ethics to supply
a *corrective* vision: the virtues we need are not those that help us
come to terms with our world, he contends, but those that help
us transform it.

May points to three images in particular that have shaped
our understanding of the physician's role. Each of these images
is helpful in certain ways, he suggests, but each is in need of the
transforming and corrective power of Christian vision. Most traditional, perhaps, is the image of the physician as *parent*. This
image has become increasingly difficult to apply in a society
shaped more by contractual than familial modes of interaction.
Moreover, the parental image has been branded as paternalistic
and severely criticized by those who see in it an affront to the
autonomy of the patient. May agrees with the criticism, but this
does not move him to become an antipaternalist; that sort of
emphasis on the autonomy of the patient, he contends, may
actually diminish the human reality of the person. "This apparent respect for autonomy actually consigns the patient to moral
oblivion. If we do not bother to judge actions, we imply that
neither the act nor the actor matters" (p. 52). And in such circumstances, physicians are likely to become technicians who do no
more than their contractual commitments require of them.

May suggests that we will not understand the physician's dilemma until we take the parental image seriously—seriously enough to see that it presents not only dangers but benefits. Conscientious parents can "crush their children in the very effort to nurture and preserve them" (p. 54). When as parents we suppress the autonomy of our children, it is often because we want above all else to protect them from suffering. We are unable to believe that any nurturant and creative influence could involve suffering. With these tendencies of the modern parent May contrasts the symbolism of baptism and intercessory prayer. In baptism we hand the child over to another, one who has suffered and died. In intercessory prayer we "relinquish an anxious control" over those for whom we pray (p. 60). And by these acts we are freed to become better providers of care. "Morally, intercession invites a carefree care for others in professional life" (p. 60).

Another prominent image of the healer is that of physician as fighter. Metaphors of war and battle dominate our understanding of disease and medicine. Here again May discerns an underlying religious stance: we stand in awe of destructive power. "The summum malum of violent death has replaced God as the effective center of religious consciousness in the modern world," he says (p. 67). As a result, we find ourselves in dilemmas from which we can see no way out. Our initial reflex is to oppose death— oppose it to the very end, with every technical possibility at our disposal. When, in turn, we recoil from the horrors such practice of medicine can inflict upon the dying, we can think of no alternative other than to embrace death as a positive good. By contrast, the context of Christian belief affirms life as a good and regards death as evil, but it relativizes both the good that is life and the evil that is death. Only God is ultimate good; hence, life need not be maintained at any cost. Death is an evil that is real but not ultimate; hence, it should be opposed, but also at some point acknowledged. We do well to battle evil, of course, but if an evil is not ultimate, it does not call for an unconditional medical struggle. Looking at death from this perspective, May suggests, we may learn to stop attempting to engineer it and learn once more to think of dying as a human act—an act which calls for certain virtues.

Perhaps most prominent in the practice of medicine today is the image of the physician as technician. The physician as parent or fighter focuses upon certain goals or ends, but the physician as technician turns means into ends. Skill in technical performance becomes the goal. "The image of the physician as fighter in a just cause recedes before the image of the technician with a justifying skill and with independent appreciation for skill tested under the fire of battle" (pp. 91-92). This is by no means entirely bad for the practice of medicine. What seems at first sight a purely aesthetic appreciation for technique can be seen to have moral implications. "Beautiful performance requires discipline" says May. "There is a right and a wrong way to do things. The wrong way usually results from a faulty technique or from an excessive preoccupation with one's ego" (p. 95). The technical image serves not only a moral but also a psychological function: it protects the fragile self of the physician, who must regularly face suffering and death. And finally, since physicians as technicians recognize a code governing good performance, the image permits a regulatory function: one's fellow practitioners must be held responsible to the code. Granting all this, however, it remains true that the image may too easily tempt physicians to think of their role as purely philanthropic: they give as purely self-sufficient givers, and patients receive as the utterly needy.

In truth, though, the physician's ability to give is not wholly gratuitous or godlike. Physicians are indebted to others for much that they have received. May suggests a better image: the physician as *covenanter*. Physicians give—and also receive. They give not just to satisfy the minimal demands of a contractual agreement but because as professionals they "profess" the healing art, because their personal identity has been shaped by the reciprocities of giving and receiving. "A covenantal ethic positions human givers in the context of a primordial act of receiving a gift not wholly deserved, which they can only assume gratefully" (p. 108). At least in relation to God, physicians are always needy and receptive, and therefore always called to gratitude. May suggests that covenants "cut deeper into personal identity" than do contracts (p. 119). There is no way for the covenanting physician, darting in and out of the patient's world of need, to keep his or her commitments limited (p. 128).

The ideal of the covenanting physician is attractive but also dangerous. It appears to call for a superhuman—and, finally, self-destructive—commitment from the physician. It is not hard to understand why a once-idealistic physician might, without base motives, retreat from such an ideal into the world of the technician. Precisely here, May suggests, the religious context of covenant imagery must not be forgotten. If covenants cut deep into personal identity, it is also true that understanding one's commitment in covenantal terms "produces an inner freedom and nonchalance that makes a deeper commitment to others tolerable" (p. 184).

> The religious tradition imparts a sense of the final extraterritoriality of the person that makes it possible to function in a "hardship post," as it were, without being annihilated thereby. One can take a job seriously precisely because one does not take it too seriously. It has not become the sole arena of self-realization. (P. 184)

The covenant image provides physicians with the corrective vision they need to see new possibilities in their commitment, and it also enables them to live with those possibilities.

To be sure, we will have to press upon May the question that concerns Hauerwas and MacIntyre: Will serious attention to the practice of medicine itself be sufficient to elicit the needed virtues of the covenanting physician? Or must we begin to wonder whether such physicians can really be developed and trained in the communities we presently inhabit? To the degree that character is shaped by community, these are questions to be taken seriously (and May does, for example, consider carefully the communities within which medical education takes place). For all the problems he sees in the practice of medicine, problems generated in large measure by the society in which that practice occurs, May does not seem ready to give up the attempt to offer society a corrective, transforming vision of virtue. Hauerwas wants to offer an alternative vision embodied in a particular community, but May wants to trace possibilities inherent in the ideals and aspirations of medicine today, and he attempts to respond to concerns medical practitioners themselves share. That the strategies are different is clear; it is less clear which of them is preferable.

IV

If the focus of our ethic turns to the agent and the agent's virtues and vices, we will soon be forced to think about the development of character. This involves us in some of the deepest religious puzzles, not always satisfactorily addressed by those who write of virtue.[18] For example, Hauerwas emphasizes "narrative" as an important category for understanding moral agency, suggesting that we know ourselves as selves only in terms of narrative. Our actions become part of a story that we make our own through the power of attention and intention (PK, 41). The self is a story, he says, and the construction of that narrative is a gradual process. But how do we see to it that our constructed self is virtuous? Imitation of moral exemplars is crucial, he says; for the Christian, imitation of Jesus is the road to virtue. Still, a problem remains. "No one can become virtuous merely by doing what virtuous people do. We can only be virtuous by doing what virtuous people do in the manner that they do it" (PK, 76). But clearly, we cannot do that until we are virtuous. Suddenly an unbridgeable chasm opens before us. The slow, laborious achievement of virtue requires imitation of those already virtuous, but imitation alone will never make one virtuous. We must imitate the exemplar by doing the deed in a virtuous manner. We can get to virtue only by first being virtuous! Nothing Hauerwas says really addresses this conundrum. Some Christians hold that grace justifies the sinner and provides the bridge across this chasm, but Hauerwas is reluctant to talk that way.

" 'Sanctification' is but a way of reminding us of the kind of journey we must undertake if we are to make the story of Jesus our story," he says. " 'Justification' is but a reminder of the character of that story—namely, what God has done for us by providing us with a path to follow" (PK, 94). Jesus is the exemplar; he provides the path to follow. But how will we learn to tread that path in the manner that he did? Something more powerful than mere example is necessary to transform the self.

This point is corroborated by a writer not usually considered "religious." In 1959, E. B. White published his revised edition of Elements of Style, by William Strunk, Jr. The resulting hybrid has been widely used in the teaching of writing and is perhaps the only interesting grammar text ever written. But the chapter on writing that White added, called "An Approach to

---

18. I address this problem at greater length in The Theory and Practice of Virtue (Notre Dame, Ind.: University of Notre Dame Press, 1984).

Style," is in certain ways a little treatise about virtue as well.[19] White suggests—and it is a provocative thought for teachers— that character is to some extent revealed in writing: "Every writer, by the way he uses the language, reveals something of his spirit, his habits, his capacities, his bias."[20] Indeed, good writing will require certain habits of behavior, a certain kind of attentiveness and self-discipline. White states that "the act of composition, or creation, disciplines the mind; writing is one way to go about thinking, and the practice and habit of writing not only drain the mind but supply it, too" (p. 70). He seems quite serious about this; at any rate, his biographer drives home the point:

> In talking about the relationship between the character of the writer and his style, White implies that if style is the man, you may change your character to some extent by changing your style. For in the process of trying to say clearly what you mean, or know, or think you know, you learn; and as you learn, you shape your character, for you are what you have learned.[21]

And yet, there is something more to good writing than attentiveness to grammar, syntax, and spelling. Were it no more than that, good writing could easily be taught—just as virtue could be taught if it were nothing more than habits of behavior that regularly issued in certain specifiable deeds. But White indicates that there is "no infallible guide to good writing" (p. 66). "Who can confidently say what ignites a certain combination of words, causing them to explode in the mind?" (p. 66) His example is compelling: "These are the times that try men's souls." Eight short, easy words put together in a simple sentence. But suppose, White says, we rewrite the sentence in other grammatically correct ways.

> Times like these try men's souls.
> How trying it is to live in these times!
> These are trying times for men's souls.
> Soulwise, these are trying times.

---

19. My attention was first called to this by Scott Elledge in his recent book, *E. B. White: A Biography* (New York: W. W. Norton, 1984). See especially Elledge's comments on pp. 328-30.

20. White, in the third revised edition of *The Elements of Style*, by William Strunk, Jr. (New York: Macmillan, 1979). Subsequent references to this work will be cited parenthetically in the text.

21. Elledge, *E. B. White*, p. 329.

What makes Thomas Paine's sentence memorable in a way the variations are not? What makes the sentence more than a grammatically and syntactically correct collection of its elements? If we could answer that question, we might be able to say what makes the virtuous self more than a collection of virtuous deeds, what gives virtue its manner or style. "Style has no such separate entity; it is nondetachable, unfilterable" (p. 69).

White's "approach" to style may trouble the student who simply wants to learn to write well. On the one hand, White tells us that learning to write clearly may impart a characteristic style to our writing. On the other, he assures us that style, though not separable from the mechanics of writing, is not an added dimension but characterizes the whole. It cannot simply be built up from attention to mechanics. If the student becomes perplexed at such advice, he may then be ready to consider the way White concludes his essay. Commenting on two especially excellent lines in a poem by Robert Louis Stevenson, White suggests the secret. The writer who hopes to write good prose must be "sustained and elevated by the power of his purpose, armed with the rules of grammar" (p. 85). But more will be needed. Stevenson, *in a moment of felicity*, wrote of a cow "blown by all the winds that pass / And wet with all the showers," and the gift of such a felicitous moment was good writing. Suddenly "one cow, out of so many, received the gift of immortality. Like the steadfast writer, she is at home in the wind and the rain; and, thanks to one moment of felicity, she will live on and on" (p. 85). The gulf between good mechanics and true style is bridged only in that moment of felicity. Elledge reports that on one occasion, when asked to give advice to young writers, White responded "Be lucky." Perhaps that will do; if not, we may need to use slightly different language, as Elledge himself does when trying to hold together White's emphases on both the teaching of writing and the need for felicity:

> White's parting explanation, that good writing occurs in moments of felicity, does not undercut his instruction in the art of writing well. It only reminds the reader that though an approach to style can be taught, the achievement of memorable writing is a miracle. To be sincere he had to say so.[22]

---

22. Elledge, *G. B. White*, p. 330.

ing to recognize their
uch a relationship, par-
ic consequences, some-
h, sometimes for third
job dealing with such
ip and assigning rights
, individuals drafting a
uebec have urged the
a scandalous proposal,
using the law to com

als only through orders
for saying that virtue is
n scope to be consistent
too narrow in scope to
bution of social ameni-
y with the tragic side of

rudimentary technical
couraging behavior be-
unishing those who fail
s ways of discouraging
rovide financial incen-
e away financial incen-
gators by forbidding the
onduct that it would be
requiring health warn-
g cigarette advertising
he pursuit of virtue and
merely historical. It has
well abandon it.

not all of our problems
people to virtue. It will
encouraging standards
ions of the freedom of
dards. The prohibition
considered an interfer-
nor does a law against
a worker's freedom to

ents and proxy solicita-

And to be likewise sincere, religious thinkers may need to
say the same about virtue. This brings us, of course, to a very old
problem: the place of grace in the moral life. The importance of
communities for shaping character is affirmed by Gustafson and
emphasized more strongly by MacIntyre and Hauerwas. And no
one can deny that character is shaped in narrative fashion, bit-by-
bit, in the communities that mold us. But if true virtue requires
more—not just a "doing" but a manner or style—we may also be
in need of recurring moments of felicity, a truth perhaps best
captured by May's covenantal emphasis. This suggests themes
that religious thinkers, more than any others, might well develop.
The need for grace, for moments of felicity, cuts deeper than the
choice between Gustafson's inner withdrawal, Hauerwas's communal withdrawal, or May's affirmation and transformation of
larger communities. For if grace is necessary, there must be limits
to any communal shaping of character.

Successful moral education probably requires a community
that does not hesitate to inculcate virtue in the young, that does
not settle for discordant opinions and alternative visions of the
good, that worries (as Plato did) about the stories its poets teach.
In short, there is likely to be little serious moral education in a
community that seeks only to be "liberal"—a point Hauerwas
presses home vigorously. At the same time, the goal of moral
education and its accompanying vision of the good can never be
fixed in advance by any community, as if it could be easily transmitted and as if no moment of felicity were required. People must
be left free to pursue and be pursued by the good, and such
pursuit may shatter the fixed vision of a community and make
moral education difficult. Communities that seek simply to remain "open" and that do not inculcate virtuous habits of behavior will utterly fail at the task of moral education. Communities
that do not permit the virtues they inculcate to be transcended
by the good will ultimately cut themselves off from the very
source that inspired their efforts to shape character. In short, the
development of true virtue requires both grace and a community
dedicated to shaping character; yet those two requirements stand
in considerable tension with each other. Perhaps communities
that seriously attempt to inculcate virtue while also gathering
regularly to confess their failures and await a moment of felicity
are the best we can manage.

On Law and Virtue

Robert E. Rodes, Jr.

Traditional teaching on the subject of law and virtue
as means to end. "The proper effect of law," says
Aquinas, "is to lead its subject to virtue." He defin
"that which makes its subject good," and describes
of good acts that grows or diminishes within us as w
to act in the way that it calls for. It follows that law
lead people to virtue—that is, to make them good—b
ing good acts and discouraging bad ones. This is the
I propose to defend in this paper.

Unfortunately, traditional doctrine couples this i
an extreme technical naivete. Medieval legal theor
firm in its perception that law must lead people to virt
limited in its understanding of how law goes about lead
anywhere. The main sources of legal material on
theory was based were the enactments by which the l
emperors tried to govern their unruly and disintegrat
and the enactments by which popes and church coun
deploy an effective ministry and make Christians be
emperors were strict and minatory, but their enforc
chinery was in tatters. The popes were firm and sente
they had no enforcement machinery at all. Furthermo
gy taught that all legal enactments were but impleme
the laws of God, and God reserves enforcement f
world. So neither emperors nor popes did much thin

we might at least punish them by refu
relationship legally. But the breakup of
ticularly after a long time, often has trag
times for one party, sometimes for bot
parties as well. The law can do a bette
situations by recognizing the relationsh
and duties in consequence. To this end
new Civil Code for the Province of Q
creation of a status of de facto marriage-
I imagine, in the eyes of those who favo
mand virtue and punish vice.

In short, if the law can pursue its g
backed by threats, there is a strong case
the wrong goal to pursue. It is too broad i
with a proper concern with freedom. It i
be helpful in the enhancement and distr
ties. It is too rigid to deal compassionatel
people's lives.

But we do not have to operate at th
level. The law has numerous ways of er
sides demanding it on the one hand and
to comply on the other. It has numerou
behavior besides punishing it. It can
tives—tax breaks for instance. It can ta
tives, as in the example of protecting alli
sale of alligator bags. It can discourage o
impossible or tyrannous to forbid—as b
ings on cigarette packages and forbiddi
on television. The correlation between
obliviousness to all these expedients is
no philosophical basis. We can perfectl

Abandoning it will solve some bu
with assigning law the function of leadin
certainly give us better opportunities fo
of behavior without unacceptable inva
people who do not live up to those sta
of cigarette advertising is not generally
ence with anyone's freedom to smoke;
paying wages in a tavern interfere wit
drink.

When it comes to wage garnishm

tion rules, though, we must take another step. The aim of measures dealing with these subjects is not to elicit specific good acts or discourage specific bad ones. It is, as I just said, to enhance social amenities and see to their just distribution. To relate this aim to the pursuit of virtue, I turn to *Gaudium et Spes*, the Second Vatican Council's Pastoral Constitution on the Church in the Modern World. Unlike earlier philosophical and theological teachings, this document links social amenities closely with human fulfillment:

> Man's social nature makes it evident that the progress of the human person and the advance of society itself hinge on each other. For the beginning, the subject, and the goal of all social institutions is and must be the human person, which for its part and by its very nature stands completely in need of social life. This social life is not something added on to man. Hence, through his dealings with others, through reciprocal duties, and through fraternal dialogue he develops all his gifts and is able to rise to his destiny.

That destiny is to be perfected in virtue. It follows, then, that virtue is the end of social life, and what I have called social amenities are society's contribution to virtue. The law's function of enhancing and distributing these amenities, therefore, is referable to its function of leading people to virtue.

Earlier sources have tended to obscure this doctrine by distinguishing too sharply between earthly and heavenly kingdoms or between our temporal and spiritual ends. However, St. Thomas moves in the direction of the doctrine when he says that if a law is properly ordered to the common good, it will tend to make people good absolutely, whereas if it is ordered to something inappropriate, it will make people good only in a narrow sense—in the sense that a man might be said to be a good robber if he knows how to rob efficiently. *Gaudium et Spes* relates this claim of St. Thomas about the common good to the claim that the law is meant to enhance social amenities by defining the common good as "the sum total of social conditions which allow people, either as groups or as individuals, to reach their fulfillment more fully and more easily."

Insofar as the enhancement and distribution of social amenities can be referred to the pursuit of virtue, so can the salvage function of law. When the law intervenes in a tragic situation, it does so to restore the social support the victims need to survive and grow—the dealings with others, reciprocal duties, and fraternal dialogue mentioned in *Gaudium et Spes*.

I believe these reflections on *Gaudium et Spes* indicate that the tenets of sociological jurisprudence can be reconciled with the claim that law should lead people to virtue. The significance of such a reconciliation depends of course on how we value sociological jurisprudence. It is a doctrine that comes out of modern technology—witness Roscoe Pound's famous metaphor of "social engineering"—and has both the strengths and the weaknesses of that technology. It offers the law a more sophisticated set of incentives and disincentives to work with than it had under the traditional notion of orders backed by threats, but it is still limited to the production of desirable behavior by manipulation of those incentives and disincentives. If law is something more than a technology for eliciting desirable patterns of behavior, then sociological jurisprudence is something less than an adequate account of it.

The technological approach has had its technological successes. It has served to enhance at crucial points the "social conditions which allow people . . . to reach their fulfillment more fully and more easily." It has put an end to a number of useless and pernicious legal dispositions from the rotten borough to the destructibility of contingent remainders. It has supported legislation abolishing the yellow-dog contract and the twelve-hour workday. It has freed the urban slum dweller from the feudal principles that made it possible for a landlord to collect rent without fixing the toilet. Its stern critique has brought about a total remodeling of civil procedure. In many ways, in short, it has served us well.

But the unrelieved pragmatism of the approach becomes destructive at the very point where the social conditions for virtue are to be translated into virtue itself. It subjects the whole legal enterprise to a rigorous bottom-line critique that it is not well able to withstand. If law is a mere instrument, it is not all that good a one. Inevitably, our ability to perceive defects and inefficiencies is more widespread and more far-reaching than our ability to cope with them. Inevitably, criticisms pile up more rapidly than reforms. From being seen as a way of getting things done, the law comes to be seen as a way of not getting things done, or as a way of getting them done badly. If people see law as nothing more than a useful tool, they will come to see it as a failure, and eventually as an enemy. They will not be able to find in it an adequate matrix for their responsibilities to one another. They will not be able to feel the moral force of society behind its dispositions or to perceive that being a good neighbor or a good citizen has anything to do with living by it.

I believe, therefore, that we cannot be content with leaving the pursuit of virtue to the bottom-line legal theories that define law by its deployment of incentives and disincentives and evaluate it in terms of its social effects. These matters are important, but they are not ultimate criteria. They must be looked at from within the context of what I call a *jurisprudence of aspirations*, by which I mean a treatment of law as an expression of what we aspire to as a community—which is not necessarily what we can realistically hope to accomplish.

If as a community we aspire to live virtuously, to deal virtuously with one another, to encourage and support one another in leading virtuous lives, then the law must bear an effective witness to the whole of that aspiration rather than merely coerce or manipulate a measure of compliance with some part. It was no sentimentalist or visionary, but the ever-practical Justice Holmes who said that "The law is the witness and external deposit of our moral life. Its history is the history of the moral development of the race. The practice of it, in spite of popular jests, tends to make good citizens and good men." If we concern ourselves only with what can or should be enforced, we overlook this function of our law, and, as a consequence, badly attenuate the moral life of our society.

Wherever there is moral concern in a social context, the law has an important role to play whether or not it can be effectively enforced. It confronts the individual conscience with the community's judgment about what is acceptable and what is to be encouraged. It offers the fruit of detached and informed moral reflection to people who have to act suddenly and under pressure. It represents the community's choice among different ways of implementing a general moral principle. As the scholastic philosophers put it, positive law makes specific what natural law (i.e., morality) leaves general.

It is through this kind of moral positioning that the law exercises much of its power to promote virtue and to support, vindicate, or protect the social conditions in which virtue can be sought. The law's massive witness against the criminal does as much to deter crime as does the fear of punishment. Poor people, if they are to live virtuously, need the community concern expressed in the welfare laws almost as much as they need the money. These are two areas in which the pragmatic approach has proved especially destructive—offering fear without moral suasion in the one case and money without compassion or respect in the other.

The task of moral positioning is complicated but not superseded by the complementary pragmatic task of deploying incentives to virtuous conduct or disincentives to the opposite. The moral positioning is often needed in circumstances where incentives and disincentives cannot be effectively deployed, and sometimes in circumstances where they cannot be justly deployed. It is especially needed in circumstances where they are being deployed in the wrong way.

Moral positioning evokes a good deal of controversy that purports to be about something else. The question of the legal status of consensual sex is often put in pragmatic terms—Is the time of the police and the prosecutor well spent in prosecuting victimless crimes?—but the real dynamic is provided by the hidden agenda of giving or not giving moral validity to the conduct in question. For my own part, I would like to see this conduct neither persecuted nor validated; I would therefore favor keeping the old laws on the books and giving them the sparse enforcement they have always had.

But it is not only in the realm of sex that there are moral principles that should not be enforced with the full power of the state but that a legal system worthy of a decent society cannot ignore. Our antitrust laws, our multiple-dwelling laws, our stock promotion laws, and especially our civil rights laws all have dispositions whose reach exceeds their grasp. Nevertheless, without them our body of law would be severely impaired in stature, and far less capable of promoting a virtuous life.

The jurisprudence of aspirations puts the relation between law and virtue on a very different footing than does the juridical triumphalism of the New Right. I have read of a judge who refuses to recite the Pledge of Allegiance to the flag on the grounds that it is not true that this nation offers "liberty and justice for all." I believe the New Right (or the Old Right for that matter) would respond, "Well maybe not all, but nearly all—if you liberals don't spoil it." Taking a strictly empirical view of the matter, I am with the judge. This is not and never has been a nation with liberty and justice for all or nearly all, and probably not even for a bare majority. But I do not take an empirical view. What makes our country special is not what it is or what it has been, but what we and generations of our predecessors have wanted and still want it to be. It is in that spirit that I recite the Pledge of Allegiance, and in the same spirit that I examine the relation between law and virtue.

As statements of what we aspire to, our laws give us no basis for congratulating ourselves. As much as they bear witness to our desire to live virtuously together, they also bear witness to how far we have fallen short of doing so. Even such technically successful measures as, say, the Fourteenth Amendment or the National Labor Relations Act are more a product of our common suffering than an excuse for complacency. Laws like these are made for use, and we often use them to good effect, but it is not their effectiveness that gives them their power to lead people to virtue. They are aspirations written in the blood of our people— at Cold Harbor and Shiloh, in Watts and Selma, in the Chicago Haymarket and in Harlan County, Kentucky. Whether we or our ancestors played a noble or an ignoble part in these confrontations, they encourage us to approach the common pursuit of virtue with a good deal of humility.

A jurisprudence of aspirations will not only prevent the development of some destructive elements in the law but will also give people a way of coping with the destructive elements that inevitably do arise. Even without accepting the traditional theory that an unjust law is no law at all, we can see the unjust use of legal forms or legal apparatus as a wound or a violence inflicted on the law. Brutal policemen, inept and uncaring bureaucrats, venal legislators, and corrupt judges make of the law not an accomplice but a victim.

Bottom-line theorists will hold that it is not acceptable to view the law as a source of moral positioning and, a fortiori, as a victim because they feel that to do so tends to bring the whole legal system into disrepute. They argue that people will lose respect for the law if they see it intruding into situations where it cannot deliver a technically effective result. This would be a serious objection if the facts bore it out. But they do not. We have whole generations of peasants, laborers, students, welfare recipients, peace demonstrators, and social activists to tell us that it is

power, not the lack of it, that causes people to lose respect for the
law.

The *locus classicus* on this question is international law.
The bottom-line critics tend to say that this body of material is
not really law at all because no one enforces it, and, indeed, when
a hard case rises, almost no one obeys it. The bottom-line objection is as persuasive here as it will ever be: we can argue about
how much we accomplish with laws against marijuana or bucket
shops, but only in the international realm can it be seriously
contended that law accomplishes nothing at all. If law does in fact
accomplish something in the international realm, where there is
neither administration nor enforcement, it must accomplish that
and more in other realms where there is even a modicum of both.

In fact, international law accomplishes a great deal—simply
by the moral positioning it affords. There are matters such as seal
hunting or the transmission of mail where it is followed by almost
everyone almost all the time. In matters such as the exploitation
of the ocean floor, governments are negotiating to set up new
rules—evidently with the intention of following them once they
are set up. Even in the heat of battle, combatants often follow the
rules of international law, accepting some military disadvantage
to do so. And where the level of compliance is not all that we
might wish, international law nonetheless provides the language
of moral discourse concerning matters to which it applies. People
claim to be following it even when they are not, and they use it
to justify their positions as best they can. Both corporations and
governments pay lawyers well to master its principles and use
them in argument.

Respect for international law seems in no way to be diminished by the impunity—indeed, the insouciance—with which it
is violated. Its vulnerability, its inability to back its moral suasion
with any kind of power, seems almost universally to be regarded
as cause for regret, not scorn. Compared with other kinds of law,
it loses nothing in public esteem from the fact that the uniformed
men who go around spreading terror are generally violating it,
not enforcing it.

My effort so far has been to restate and support the traditional doctrine that law is meant to lead people to virtue in the
light of the modern perception that it is meant to do other things—
support liberty, enhance and distribute social amenities, and help
pick up the pieces when things go wrong. I have saved for last

the most cogent objection to my doctrine—namely, the problem of who, in a pluralist society, is to decide what constitutes virtue. Who is entitled to embody the notions of virtue in the law under which we all will have to live? This is not a matter of freedom; I have already recognized that issue and accepted an obligation to respect it. Rather, the objection consists of the claim that the law must be strictly neutral regarding one version of virtue and another. It is not a claim that people outside the mainstream must be respected; it is a claim that there is no mainstream. It is not a claim for the rights of dissenters; it is a claim that there is nothing to dissent from.

Before looking at this claim philosophically, we should note that its consequences are pernicious. First, it deprives us of any basis for imposing accountability on the people who are running our country. It radically privatizes all values. And without public values, we have no way of challenging what business people, administrators, doctors, soldiers, and (alas!) lawyers are doing with their professional skills.

The claim is also pernicious in that it exposes people to harmful social influences that the law has no way of countering. It is possible for the law to be neutral regarding different notions of virtue, but it is hardly possible for a whole society to be. People make decisions about how they will live in the midst of a welter of conflicting social influences. The question is whether and to what extent one of those influences will be the law. If we try to remove the law from this catalogue of influences, there will be no lack of candidates for the vacancy it leaves—and a good many will be more dangerous than the law.

The philosophical grounding for this baneful privatization of values seems to be jointly attributable to Descartes and Hume. Mainstream Western philosophy took from Descartes the view that beyond sense data nothing can be affirmed with certainty except logical deductions from self-evident principles, and from Hume it received the view that value judgments cannot be derived from sense data. From these premises, it has generally been concluded that value judgments are matters of mere personal preference on the order of liking or not liking parsnips. A corollary is that the law has no more reason to be concerned with values than with whether or not people eat parsnips. For two centuries political and legal philosophers have been trying to avoid this conclusion or mitigate its destructive consequences without abandoning the premises on which it is based. They have not succeeded.

I believe we should meet these premises head on. To do so, I would appeal to natural law. There are of course a number of different accounts of this concept on the market, but there is no need to choose one here. To overcome the privatization of values we need only recognize that we can employ connatural judgments about values (i.e., judgments arrived at through experiencing the human condition as a participant) in evaluating and shaping the law. To accept natural law is to accept that such judgments are a source of knowledge and that systematic reflection on them can yield philosophical truth.

In mainstream Catholic theology, and in those Protestant traditions that accept natural law, it is assumed that revelation guides and supports our capacity for making connatural judgments without in any way superseding it. With this approach, it is possible to maintain philosophical and theological judgments in considerable harmony, and, indeed, to maintain them without being too concerned about which is which.

Connatural judgments may legitimately be proposed as sources of values in a pluralist society because, whether they are couched in philosophical or theological terms, they are communicated on the basis of shared experiences of the human condition. They will not have consequences for the law unless they come to command something like a consensus. In fact, I think there is in our society a broader connatural consensus than we sometimes suppose. It is the philosophical privatization of values that has led us to discount that consensus and look for some other basis for our laws.

Natural law doctrine, then, with its appeal to connatural judgments as a source of value and philosophical truth, meets the prevailing philosophy on the subject head on. Advocates of the prevailing philosophy respond to this challenge with both theoretical and practical attacks on natural law doctrine.

The theoretical objection is basically circular. It is claimed that the proposition that judgments constitute a source of truth different from either logical deduction or empirical observation cannot be accepted because it is neither a logical deduction nor an empirical observation. This argument deserves much shorter shrift than it generally gets.

The practical objection is that natural law doctrine is at

once anarchic and despotic. Since the judgments to which it appeals are neither logically deducible nor empirically observable, it is impossible to get people to agree on them. If one person may legitimately impose his or her version on other people, every other person may legitimately do the same. The resulting chaos will not end until one of the contenders overcomes the others by brute force.

Experience entirely fails to bear this objection out. Certainly there have been serious and destructive disagreements about the content of natural law, but there have been equally serious and destructive disagreements about what legal principles can be logically or empirically arrived at. On the whole, shared experience of being human and shared intuitions of how human beings ought to live have commanded a broader consensus in society than any but the most rudimentary of logical deductions or empirical observations.

Nor does history support the popular view that connatural judgments have tended to support bad institutions while logical or empirical judgments have supported good ones. For instance, the nineteenth-century arguments in favor of slavery in this country were on the whole empirical, while the arguments against it were on the whole connatural. Similarly, the excesses of industrial capitalism were on the whole supported by logical or empirical reasoning and resisted on connatural grounds. The cold logic of utilitarianism was rigorously invoked in favor of laissez-faire economics, while Marx's and Engel's critiques, although they purport to be scientific, in fact bristle with connatural outrage.

In our own century, the death camp personnel and the designers and builders of gas ovens relied on the logic of obedience to superiors and the attainment of abstract goals to overcome their connatural aversion to what they were given to do. It is well known that the German legal community responded to the Nazi experience by turning almost en masse to natural law doctrine after World War II.

The key concepts for a natural law approach to the institutions of a free pluralist society are dialogue and respect. Because natural law is based on the validity of connatural judgments, and connatural judgments are communicated through shared experience, it is always possible for people to talk about points on which they differ in the light of what they have in common. At the same time, by sharing the experience of being human, they share the experience of being unique. Every person can recognize every other person as having a particular version of the common destiny to work out, the common predicament to undergo. Every person is like every other person in having his or her own ways of doing so. In this context, pluralism and the promotion of virtue go hand in hand. Just as everyone needs incentives to be good, and everyone needs guidance, so everyone needs space.

As for the question of who is to decide what constitutes virtue, the answer is that we all are. We must remember that law is primarily not a thing done but a thing said. If police officers or judges set out to make it effective, it is because they have read or heard that that is what they are supposed to do. Before we address laws and proposed laws to these officials, we address them to one another. They are the language of moral discourse in our society. Through them we offer guidance, motivation, encouragement, and space to one another and claim or accept the same at each other's hands. The process is always subtle, sometimes shrill, and never neat. But on the whole, if allowed to operate, it produces what it is meant to produce—a legally supported consensus about how we may live virtuously together without either suppressing our differences or privatizing our values. We may suppose that such a consensus, if allowed to develop freely over a long time (as it has never been), would grow closer and closer to a traditional Christian understanding of virtue. "For," we read in *Gaudium et Spes*, "the Church knows full well that her message is in harmony with the most secret desires of the human heart."

Democracy, Virtue, and Religion: A Historical Perspective

Bernard Semmel

This essay presents a view of the relationship between democracy and virtue from the standpoint of history rather than from the more familiar perspective of political philosophy. Since I deal primarily with the United States and England in the past three centuries, the role of religion is a central issue. Any effort to discuss so complex a problem in a short essay must be somewhat idiosyncratic. In this case, what may seem a surprising yoking of the doctrines of evangelical Arminianism and the perception of a democratic virtue by the leading nineteenth-century rationalist philosopher is the outcome of two studies I have made which deal with these subjects.* I discuss the difficulties confronting a regime of virtue in a pluralist democracy supported by different and at times conflicting moral bases in these volumes; in this essay it is as much as I can do merely to allude to these difficulties. A secularist might question whether believers can accept any basis for a moral life other than their own; many believers would ask the same question and proceed to argue that the idea of a freely chosen—as opposed to divinely sanctioned—virtue is specious, and the acceptance of different bases of virtue is at best patronizing.

---

* *The Methodist Revolution* (New York: Basic Books, 1973) and *John Stuart Mill and the Pursuit of Virtue* (New Haven: Yale University Press, 1984).

The traditional view of democracy from Aristotle through the nineteenth century was that the passions and interests of the ruling majority would imperil the survival of virtue and of liberty, with which virtue was often linked. The history of the ancient Greek city states and of Rome was cited as evidence. Political philosophers contended that virtue (understood as obedience to a moral standard and a preference for the public over the private good) and the liberty to assume control of one's life so as to direct it toward moral goals were more likely to flourish in an aristocratic or even a monarchical state. When such states turned to popular government, factious politics stifled liberty and undermined civic morals; soon these states could no longer manage their internal affairs or defend themselves against external enemies. They fell victim to oligarchs and despots or to foreign domination.

*   *   *

When it became clear by the end of the eighteenth century that some form of democratic government would prevail in the modern Western state, political theorists speculated about how they might avoid the fate of the ancient democracies. Montesquieu, in the spirit of the Enlightenment, described constitutional forms that would protect liberty and civic virtue, and the authors of the American Constitution devised a system of checks and balances that they hoped would prevent the interests of factions and the passions of masses from subverting the public good. However useful such a system, a number of political theorists suggested that even the best constitutional mechanisms would by themselves be inadequate. Rousseau advocated a civil religion to preserve a good society, but such a solution proved to have serious defect. In the 1770s Rousseau's disciple Robespierre executed a plan to impose a republic of virtue in which individual freedom had no place; this culminated in the worship of the goddess Liberty and the bloody fanaticism of the Reign of Terror. In the 1850s Auguste Comte proposed a religion of humanity—also designed to impose a regime of virtue—that embodied a civil religion not only hostile to individual happiness and destructive of liberty but ridiculous to all but a small group of intellectuals.

A contemporary of Comte, the liberal democrat John Stuart Mill, rejected the French positivist's vision of an imposed virtue

And to be likewise sincere, religious thinkers may need to say the same about virtue. This brings us, of course, to a very old problem: the place of grace in the moral life. The importance of communities for shaping character is affirmed by Gustafson and emphasized more strongly by MacIntyre and Hauerwas. And no one can deny that character is shaped in narrative fashion, bit-by-bit, in the communities that mold us. But if true virtue requires more—not just a "doing" but a manner or style—we may also be in need of recurring moments of felicity, a truth perhaps best captured by May's covenantal emphasis. This suggests themes that religious thinkers, more than any others, might well develop. The need for grace, for moments of felicity, cuts deeper than the choice between Gustafson's inner withdrawal, Hauerwas's communal withdrawal, or May's affirmation and transformation of larger communities. For if grace is necessary, there must be limits to any communal shaping of character.

Successful moral education probably requires a community that does not hesitate to inculcate virtue in the young, that does not settle for discordant opinions and alternative visions of the good, that worries (as Plato did) about the stories its poets teach. In short, there is likely to be little serious moral education in a community that seeks only to be "liberal"—a point Hauerwas presses home vigorously. At the same time, the goal of moral education and its accompanying vision of the good can never be fixed in advance by any community, as if it could be easily transmitted and as if no moment of felicity were required. People must be left free to pursue and be pursued by the good, and such pursuit may shatter the fixed vision of a community and make moral education difficult. Communities that seek simply to remain "open" and that do not inculcate virtuous habits of behavior will utterly fail at the task of moral education. Communities that do not permit the virtues they inculcate to be transcended by the good will ultimately cut themselves off from the very source that inspired their efforts to shape character. In short, the development of true virtue requires both grace and a community dedicated to shaping character; yet those two requirements stand in considerable tension with each other. Perhaps communities that seriously attempt to inculcate virtue while also gathering regularly to confess their failures and await a moment of felicity are the best we can manage.

On Law and Virtue

Robert E. Rodes, Jr.

Traditional teaching on the subject of law and virtue relates them as means to end. "The proper effect of law," says St. Thomas Aquinas, "is to lead its subject to virtue." He defines virtue as "that which makes its subject good," and describes it as a habit of good acts that grows or diminishes within us as we act or fail to act in the way that it calls for. It follows that law is meant to lead people to virtue—that is, to make them good—by encouraging good acts and discouraging bad ones. This is the insight that I propose to defend in this paper.

Unfortunately, traditional doctrine couples this insight with an extreme technical naivete. Medieval legal theory was very firm in its perception that law must lead people to virtue but very limited in its understanding of how law goes about leading people anywhere. The main sources of legal material on which this theory was based were the enactments by which the late Roman emperors tried to govern their unruly and disintegrating empire and the enactments by which popes and church councils tried to deploy an effective ministry and make Christians behave. The emperors were strict and minatory, but their enforcement machinery was in tatters. The popes were firm and sententious, but they had no enforcement machinery at all. Furthermore, theology taught that all legal enactments were but implementations of the laws of God, and God reserves enforcement for another world. So neither emperors nor popes did much thinking about ways of enforcing their policies. They contented themselves with giving their orders and respectively beheading or excommunicating such violators as they caught. Reflecting on the available material, then, medieval legal scholars viewed law as simply a set of rules and precepts (do this, don't do that) backed by the threat— often the idle threat—of punishment. None of them would have thought, for instance, to protect alligators by suppressing the sale of alligator bags instead of by increasing the punishment for poaching.

At this technical level, the pursuit of virtue cannot be reconciled with the legitimate expectations that a modern pluralistic society has for its legal system. In the first place, it cannot be reconciled with freedom for those who do not accept the prevailing notions of virtue or do not choose to live up to them. If law is nothing more than a set of orders backed by threats, then every legal intervention is *pro tanto* a restriction of freedom, and law has no way of supporting freedom except by limiting the range of its interventions. The pursuit of virtue gives it too broad a range to leave any room for freedom.

Furthermore, perhaps the major concern of a modern legal system is that social amenities be enhanced and equitably distributed. Commanding virtuous behavior and punishing disobedience is a wholly inadequate response to this concern. Paying debts is virtuous, as is paying wages promptly, and providing relief to the poor. How then can the goal of virtue tell us whether to let a creditor garnish a worker's wages? We must move from questions of virtue to questions of labor relations and consumer credit before we can deal intelligently with the subject. And even if reflections on virtue can shed some light on consumer credit, what can they tell us about the content of the Securities and Exchange Commission's proxy solicitation rules?

Another more personal legal function that is hard to bring within the principle of commanding virtuous acts under suitable penalties is salvage. Many of the law's interventions into people's lives are calculated not to make them be good but to pick up the pieces after they have been bad or after someone else has treated them badly. Persistent moralizing is destructive to this function. Take, for instance, the cohabitation of the unmarried. An unvarnished pursuit of virtue through orders backed by threats would call for legislation banning this practice and punishing anyone caught at it. If we were not ready to fill our jails with such people, we might at least punish them by refusing to recognize their relationship legally. But the breakup of such a relationship, particularly after a long time, often has tragic consequences, sometimes for one party, sometimes for both, sometimes for third parties as well. The law can do a better job dealing with such situations by recognizing the relationship and assigning rights and duties in consequence. To this end, individuals drafting a new Civil Code for the Province of Quebec have urged the creation of a status of de facto marriage—a scandalous proposal, I imagine, in the eyes of those who favor using the law to command virtue and punish vice.

In short, if the law can pursue its goals only through orders backed by threats, there is a strong case for saying that virtue is the wrong goal to pursue. It is too broad in scope to be consistent with a proper concern with freedom. It is too narrow in scope to be helpful in the enhancement and distribution of social amenities. It is too rigid to deal compassionately with the tragic side of people's lives.

But we do not have to operate at this rudimentary technical level. The law has numerous ways of encouraging behavior besides demanding it on the one hand and punishing those who fail to comply on the other. It has numerous ways of discouraging behavior besides punishing it. It can provide financial incentives—tax breaks for instance. It can take away financial incentives, as in the example of protecting alligators by forbidding the sale of alligator bags. It can discourage conduct that it would be impossible or tyrannous to forbid—as by requiring health warnings on cigarette packages and forbidding cigarette advertising on television. The correlation between the pursuit of virtue and obliviousness to all these expedients is merely historical. It has no philosophical basis. We can perfectly well abandon it.

Abandoning it will solve some but not all of our problems with assigning law the function of leading people to virtue. It will certainly give us better opportunities for encouraging standards of behavior without unacceptable invasions of the freedom of people who do not live up to those standards. The prohibition of cigarette advertising is not generally considered an interference with anyone's freedom to smoke; nor does a law against paying wages in a tavern interfere with a worker's freedom to drink.

When it comes to wage garnishments and proxy solicita-

that treated individuality as a prime enemy. Like Hamilton and Madison, Mill saw the utility of constitutional mechanisms and advocated a system of representation to guarantee that the ablest and best-educated (whom he believed would more readily respond to moral appeals) would not be swamped by an unenlightened majority concerned only with material happiness. But he understood that such a device would not by itself protect liberty or preserve virtue in a mass society that insisted on conformity, in a commercial society that held selfish interest as its principal criterion. Mill turned to the individual conscience—not divinely installed but instilled by an appropriate education—to serve as a moral guide, and he called for the pursuit of a higher happiness in a *freely chosen* virtue in self-dependence and self-development as well as a readiness to respond to social obligation.

This was a rather grand moral ambition for a mass democracy, and it would clearly be difficult to realize. The French historian and political philosopher Alexis de Tocqueville, a friend of Mill, believed that the necessary basis for a society at once virtuous and democratic lay not in the man-made conscience Mill was proposing but in a willing subordination to divine authority. In his study of democracy in America, Tocqueville declared that "despotism may be able to do without faith, but freedom cannot." He held the issue to be crucial. "How could society escape destruction if, when political ties are relaxed, moral ties are not tightened, and what can be done with a people master of itself if it is not subject to God?" The French elite in the eighteenth century had given up its religion, and its efforts to create a secular faith during the Revolution had ended in anarchy and terror. In the decades following, bureaucratic despotism and intermittent social upheavals continued to put liberty at risk. England and the United States were more fortunate. For what Tocqueville called "Anglo-American civilization" was uniquely the "product" of "two perfectly distinct elements which elsewhere have often been at war with one another. . . . I mean," he concluded, "the *spirit of religion* and the *spirit of freedom.*"

What was the source of this Anglo-American faith? The Puritan revolution of the seventeenth century had delivered a somewhat ambiguous message, for its call to freedom was often muffled by an insistence on man's powerlessness. If all were predetermined and salvation depended entirely on God's grace, how could one speak of liberty? The eighteenth century saw the be-

ginnings in both Great Britain and the American colonies of
what has become known as the Great Revival. Though a number
of evangelists continued to preach the Calvinist gospel of the
Puritans, John Wesley and his followers conjoined a churchly
Arminianism to a sectarian evangelism. Wesley's Methodists
spoke of a freedom of will in place of a Calvinist predestination,
of the possibility of salvation for all in place of the Calvinist
doctrine of the election of a small minority. God had endowed
us with sufficient liberty that we might by our own efforts achieve
salvation, they insisted. Without denying mankind's inherent
limitations, and always stressing the necessity of divine grace,
Wesley went so far as to speak of the possibility of achieving
spiritual perfection in this life. Before the end of the century, the
principal doctrines of this evangelical Arminianism had pene-
trated the practical beliefs of almost all the denominations of
Anglo-American Protestantism.

What meaning did this gospel have for democracy? Certain
present-day historians have argued that Western society in the
last quarter of the eighteenth and first quarter of the nineteenth
century was prepared to embrace modern democratic goals. In
France, social revolution served as the vehicle transmitting these
ideals; on the European continent it was the conquering armies
of the French republic and then of Napoleon; in the New World
it was anticolonial rebellions; in England it was a conjunction of
America's war of independence and the enthusiasm of the Great
Revival. In the doctrines of free will and universal salvation
explicit in the Arminian theology and implicit in any movement
of mass evangelization were appeals to liberty and equality—the
political faith that a modern industrial society required. Nor
could so radical a change be produced routinely or accepted
perfunctorily. The pervasive enthusiasm of the Revival was necessary to make "new men." Moreover, Wesleyan preachers, soon
imitated by those of other denominations, organized religious
associations that helped to endow ordinary men and women with
a sense of worth and to support their efforts to attain spiritual
perfection, thus adding fraternity to the democratic compound—
an essential element in a society racked by dislocations of population and the new industrialism.

In eighteenth-century France the religious skepticism of
the intellectual elite and the governing classes triumphed over
revealed religion, but Tocqueville observed that the "religious

instinct" continued to have "its most abiding home in the hearts of the common people." Ordinary men and women needed a faith and turned to that of the Revolution, which according to Tocqueville "created an atmosphere of missionary fervor and, indeed, assumed all the aspects of a religious revival." Like such revivals, the Revolution wished to produce not only "new men" but also the "regeneration of the whole human race." In France, this regeneration proved to be a bloody business. On the other hand, in England and America the democratic revolution transpired with a minimum of bloodshed, and it managed to flourish and endure. This may have been the result of the earlier religious revival incorporating in its doctrine and the methods by which it mobilized popular energies on behalf of personal salvation a spiritual version of the new democratic faith. In this attenuated form, the enthusiasm that elsewhere led to libertinism and anarchy instead helped to bring great masses to a pursuit of virtue, to self-discipline and an ordered liberty.

Modern democratic and industrial society required what religious faith made accessible to the ordinary people of England and America. The Arminian appeal to justification by works as well as by faith encouraged millions to seek self-improvement and equipped them with the discipline and assurance necessary to play active parts in society, even as their participation in religious associations gave them the necessary practice. The revival of religion helped to transform great numbers from the passivity that characterized the traditional community to relative self-dependence, and it also made available the disciplined energies of previously untapped sections of the population to an expanding industrialism and a democratic polity.

* * *

But even if religion did powerfully assist the great transformation required to make modern men and women, the new liberal and industrial society gradually came to the conclusion that revealed religion had been invalidated by scientific advances. At first this growing conviction undermined not so much faith in a Creator and loyalty to what we may call the Judeo-Christian moral tradition but rather the premodern confidence that whoever did not share the beliefs or follow the forms of a particular denomination was doomed to perdition. Indeed, the new democratic pluralism could not have prospered had the old sectarian bigotry survived. However, what began as the necessary exercise of tolerance of different approaches to an understanding and worship of God, accompanied as they were by an adherence to a common moral standard, became not only a denial of God's existence but a denial also of the validity of any set of moral principles.

In a secular democracy, many argued, all individuals possess the right to follow the moral precepts of their choice. Observers in the social sciences noted that various non-Western cultures held different ideas of right and wrong, and they concluded that it was therefore foolish to claim that the Judeo-Christian standard was superior. Within limits defined by the law, they believed, the motto of Rabelais's Abbey of Theleme—"Do what thou wilt"— ought to prevail, and political pressure and changing standards impelled legislation and shaped judicial decisions to expand these limits. Everything was relative; only mankind's subordination to the necessities of our animal nature was certain. A reasoned antinomianism (i.e. selective opposition to the moral law), previously the preserve of fringe groups, became a part of the civil religion of a democratic and secular West. A system of secondary and higher schools reaching out to a greater proportion of youth than ever before abandoned a part of its earlier educational task in favor of redeeming students from the "superstition" and retrogressive moral rigidity inculcated by ignorant parents. With moral restraints removed, and assisted by the new possibilities afforded by science, men and women in western democracies were encouraged to satisfy, if not sate, sensual and material appetites without hindrance.

Is such a defeat of virtue, as traditionally defined, inevitable in a democratic and secular society? Despairing of democratic politics, we have noted that the ancient philosophers believed that public morals were imperiled by a popular Epicureanism. John Stuart Mill similarly denounced the modern democrat's overriding concern for physical happiness; he spoke of a commercial society's concentration on "money-getting" and condemned the moral cowardice of its elite. According to Mill, Bentham and his followers had no understanding of "the most natural and strongest feelings of human nature." The idea that a human being—"that most complex being"—might be "capable of pursuing spiritual perfection as an end" was foreign to them, he suggested. They failed to recognize "the existence of conscience" as distinct from self-interest or a concern for public opinion, and they were unaware that "self-respect" or "honour" or "personal dignity" could serve as motives for action. For many who thought themselves democrats, liberty was of little importance, and the traditional values of loyalty and duty were simply the relics of a decaying aristocracy. Courage and a "self-relying independence" were encountered less often, and "the refined classes" were marked by "a moral effeminacy" and "an ineptitude for every kind of struggle."

Liberal philosophers have been divided into schools of utilitarians on the one hand and those who defend individual rights on the other. It was Mill's complaint that the former—those who adopt Bentham's calculus of pleasures and pains and the criterion of the greatest happiness for the greatest number—have no persuasive moral basis. Although Mill favored free choice by individuals so long as no injury was done to others, he insisted on distinctions between higher and lower forms of happiness. Unlike Bentham, he would not concede that the child's game of pushpin is as good as poetry. Mill argued that Bentham's crude effort to attain the general good by catering to appetites had to be subordinated to a moral and social end—what Mill called "utility in the largest sense, grounded in the permanent interest of man as a progressive being." Proponents of the second variety of liberal philosophy, usually identified with Kant, were critical of the fact that Bentham's utilitarianism neglects inherent human rights; this school sought to treat individuals as ends in themselves and believed it wrong to attempt to direct people to a particular way of life. Mill's call for self-development owed much to this German philosophy, but it did not prevent him from warning that a life lived in isolation or given up entirely to self-interest diminished both individuality and liberty. Individuals have pressing common goals, and in the tradition of the ancient philosophers, Mill wished to educate men and women to make of their own volition such sacrifices for the public interest as might be necessary without subjecting themselves to an ethic of self-denial for its own sake. Only if individuals were guided by a voluntarily accepted sense of rectitude and moral duty in developing their capacities, Mill insisted, could a society remain both free and virtuous. "And hence it is said with truth," he wrote, following the Stoics and the German idealist philosophers, "that none but a person of confirmed virtue is completely free." Or, he added elsewhere, truly happy.

*   *   *

Mill's fears for democratic society have largely been realized in our century. Social scientists, convinced that their expertise could bring about a utopian era of social and individual happiness, more and more attributed mankind's ills not to our own defects or to the human condition but to a remediable malfunctioning of society. If evil or vice exists, society—the family, the churches, the state—is to blame. The effect has been to foster a new paternalism, to promote an increased dependence on classes of social professionals and upon the state rather than, in Mill's words, genuinely "to aid individuals in the formation of their own character" and to help them call upon the inner moral resources that lead to self-dependence.

John Maynard Keynes, hardly a fervent defender of traditional morality, describes the dominant Benthamite liberalism of our time with its "overvaluation of the economic criterion" in depicting human beings as mere creatures of material necessity as "the worm which has been gnawing at the insides of modern civilization and is responsible for its present moral decay." A determinist and materialist Marxism is the heir to this Benthamism, and it, along with a crude Freudianism that describes human beings as mere puppets of their animal natures, has become the governing creeds of the age. A psychological behavioralism of the sort promoted by B. F. Skinner derides the human freedom and dignity advocated by Mill and others. Those who uphold traditional values, Skinner charges, foolishly vaunt man as "a moral hero" possessing "inner virtues" and engaged in a grand "moral struggle"; Skinner, on the other hand, dismisses the idea of virtue in order "to make life less punishing."

The movement of modern society away from virtue—whether defined in terms of the aristocratic code, traditional Judeo-Christian morality, or self-dependence—has become yet more evident in the past decade. For the better-placed and more articulate classes of the Western democracies, as Mill early perceived, a moral and physical timidity conjoined to an electoral and financial advantage to prevent any effective opposition to this decline. At home, fear and guilt inhibit individual autonomy, and politicians of both parties have made self-reliance for businesses and individuals alike appear outmoded and foolish. The definition of the generally accepted values of diversity and opportunity for all has been distorted to enlarge further the area of dependence. A commercial and democratic society insists on its right to merchandise all goods; the appeal to traditional values in the attempt to restrain pornography, for example, is regarded as a "reactionary" violation of a scientifically validated cultural relativism as well as of the First Amendment. Abroad, we see expansionist states that have destroyed the liberties of their own peoples and threaten those of others. So far have timidity and narrow commercial interest taken us that anyone who suggests that it may be suicidal to give such states the means to achieve their goals is at best considered innocent of the necessities of international trade and at worst considered an advocate of a nuclear holocaust or, somewhat better, a troglodyte still clinging to a belief in the existence of evil. This passivity and the desire for ease and profits are usually masked by appeals to guilt because of Western affluence, to historical or geopolitical inevitability, or to an undeniably moral if frighteningly one-sided regard for international law. All this threatens not merely virtue, democracy, and liberty, but our very survival.

The goal of a freely chosen virtue is clearly difficult to achieve. Marxist-Leninists offer the alternative of a state-imposed virtue—a society in which individuality in all its forms is subordinated to an oligarchic determination of what is socially necessary. In such a state, virtue means moral and physical servitude. The only hope for a mass democracy remains the alliance of "the spirit of religion and the spirit of freedom" that Tocqueville wrote about a century and a half ago. Such a union provides a realistic basis for a voluntarily adopted virtue on the part of millions—a virtue that can rescue liberal democracies from self-destructive social and economic illusions and also prepare them for the long period of patient confrontation with the enemies of liberty that constitutes our only hope for preserving peace with them.

This is not a sermon advocating a religious revival. The revival has already begun, and it is likely to grow in force. What kind of movement will it prove to be? In eighteenth- and nineteenth-century America and England such a spiritual awakening assisted the assimilation of modern liberal values and the establishment of a vigorous industrial and democratic society. However, history offers many examples of religious eruptions that ignited bigotry, fanaticism, and rampant violence; such an eventuality might prove even more destructive of civilized life today. If the present revival follows such a course, there will be no room for either virtue or liberal democracy. We must hope for an awakening similar to that mounted by the Anglo-American evangelists of the eighteenth century, one that would at the same time satisfy spiritual longings, rout antinomian passions, and engender an enthusiasm for virtue and an ordered liberty. The alternative may be a totalitarian state that has its own means of dealing with the frustrations that modern society, bereft of a sense of community and of spiritual and moral values, gives rise to.

Great numbers can only be reached by enthusiasm, the poet and novelist Oliver Goldsmith declared at the time of the earlier revival. What the church and the statesmen of England had to do, he observed, was "conspire with their enthusiasms." While noting the dangers they might pose, Goldsmith insisted on the usefulness of heightened religious emotions in "improving society," in giving men and women a sense of their own worth and of community. If the church and the governing classes joined and guided this effusion of powerful feelings, he concluded, England would be "the happiest nation on earth," for "a society of enthusiasts governed by reason among the great, is the most indissoluble" and "the most virtuous . . . that can be imagined." Today, even a rationalist of the Mill school, more and more convinced of the limitations of the naked human condition, can see the force of arguments long made by believers and appreciate the utility of Goldsmith's counsel.

Exploring Virtue: A
Report on a Conversation

The more than twenty people addressing the subject of "Virtue—Public and Private" included academics, journalists, philosophers, theologians, a foundation executive, and a civil servant. Virtue is a subject that came easily to the sturdy Dutch burghers whose presence is evoked by the dark oaken decor of the conference room of the University Club in New York City. Virtue, either as topic of conversation or conscious habit, seems somewhat exotic in the 1980s. Nonetheless, virtue, or at least the idea of virtue, is making something of a comeback, as evidenced by the liveliness of this two-day discussion.

The four papers that framed the discussion are included in this volume. They framed the discussion, but they did not rigidly confine it, for the occasional flow and frequent eruptions of agreements and disagreements could not be contained within a neatly segmented quartet of subtopics. Each presentor took the time assigned to go beyond the argument of his original paper. James Billington of the Woodrow Wilson Center, for example, strongly emphasized the existence of a cultural crisis centered in a lack of virtue and virtue-forming institutions. Billington knows that you shouldn't have to call a conference to discover that the world could do with a great deal more virtue. That there is never enough virtue in the world would seem to be self-evident. Our crisis consists in the fact that we need to make arguments, present evidence, and even call conferences to point out the self-evident.

The crisis, said Billington, is evident in our addiction to "freedom without responsibility." Those who would dismiss this as a cliche ought first to try to urge its truth upon the "university-media complex," where it meets with the stiffest resistance. Colleges, universities, and the communications media typically "fail to transmit or exemplify the basic traditions, the value-forming traditions, of American life," he said, "and most especially those traditions rooted in religion." Indeed, these institutions are doing exactly the opposite, often quite deliberately so. Where these institutions do claim to be transmitting "values," the values transmitted are usually antitraditional, ahistorical, and morally undemanding.

A century ago, the well-to-do might have promoted a foreign missionary society or engaged in settlement house work among the poor. The functional equivalent of that today, said Billington, is to be a patron of the opera or of an art exhibit. Art has become "the vaguely sanctifying force" for the American elite. It supplies the satisfaction of feeling morally superior without making inconvenient moral demands. At this point Peter Berger suggested that this, as our Marxist friends say, is no accident. Moral judgments, like most everything else, can be reduced to a matter of taste, there being nothing so subjective as aesthetic appreciations.

Billington produced further illustrations of his point from the university scene. Tenure committees, he noted, seldom raise a question about a professional candidate's ability to serve as a "role model" for students. He recalled one occasion on which that question was raised. It was met by a you've-got-to-be-kidding incredulity. The idea of virtue is virtually ignored by the university, until perhaps it crops up at graduation ceremonies. Then there may be some inflated language about graduates being ready to assume their "moral responsibility" as citizens. Not infrequently a professor might be lauded for his or her "moral leadership," meaning, more likely than not, his activism in the "protest culture." But the dominant reality is illustrated, said Billington, by what happened when a foundation called a conference on higher education and values. A number of smaller colleges, mainly church-related colleges, responded, but not one major university sent a representative. On most prestige campuses—and on a good many that are not so prestigious—Nietzsche is rated as more important reading than Jeremiah or Saint Paul. These,

Billington argued, are but a few of the evidences supporting the proposition that, as a society, we are indeed in cultural crisis.

Robert Rodes of the Notre Dame Law School did not disagree, but he urged the conference to focus on the evolution of professional classes as a cause of the crisis. The crisis has been brought about not so much by society, he argued, as by the professions, which have with increasing success shielded themselves from accountability to society. The professions represented in the "university-media complex" have reinforced their nonaccountability by acquiring technical and organizational skills that make a reformist challenge almost impossible. (Rodes said this partly in defense of Billington, who had been criticized for being long on analysis but short on solutions.) It is hard to solve a problem, said Rodes, when the professional problem-solvers have an interest in perpetuating the problem. The specialness of the professional specialists is jeopardized if they are perceived to be part of the same cultural stream in which nonspecialists swim.

C. Eric Lincoln of Duke University picked up on this point. There is, he noted, a venerable and perfectly honorable tradition that suggests that the university should be a place of "elevated conversation." The universities ought to deal with the "great ideas" that have preoccupied thoughtful people for centuries. Historically this university discourse has been assumed to be the elevated dimension of a common tradition. "There was a body of doctrine," said Lincoln, "often church doctrine, which was simply assumed to be a source of virtue." But now, he said, the university typically feels no obligation to that common tradition, or perhaps to any tradition. In fact, even spontaneity is thought to be a source of virtue equal to any other. The result, he concluded, is a "free-market model of virtue."

Bernard Semmel of the State University of New York, Stony Brook, suggested that this did not "just happen" and that it cannot be explained adequately by reference to professionalizing self-interest alone, although that's part of the explanation. He pointed to a "university culture," which is quite consciously competing with the "home culture" of the students. It has become part of the very idea of getting a university education to "transcend" the usually middle-class values received from the family, the church, or other "less elevated" institutions. To be properly educated is to be liberated from the common culture—which is depicted as being, well . . . common.

Semmel's argument met with strong agreement from James Nuechterlein of Valparaiso University. In his years of university teaching in Canada and the United States, said Nuechterlein, he had been struck by the "self-delusion" of fellow teachers who think their great challenge is to "de-ideologize" their students and open them up to "critical thinking." "In my experience, very few students come to us with heavy ideological baggage which we must help them to get rid of," said Nuechterlein. "On the contrary, most of them are 'mindless relativists' without an idea in their heads other than the idea that all ideas are relative. They automatically assume that tolerance is the highest virtue and that ideals below almighty tolerance are all more or less equal." According to Nuechterlein, the task of the university today is not so much to relativize the absolutes that students have inherited but to help move them toward reflection beyond the absolute of relativity. Students are open to the importance of reason and conscience, he asserted, but it is not so easy to persuade them that there is such a thing as *right* reason and *informed* conscience.

But we should not lay all the blame on the university, Brian Benestad of Scranton University urged. The university is just one among several culture-forming institutions, and they all have similar problems in talking about virtue in public. Even in institutions where you would expect the question of virtue to be addressed, it is not. Benestad cited the Roman Catholic bishops' pastoral letter "The Challenge of Peace: God's Promise and Our Response." "Among the many remarkable things about that pastoral," said Benestad, "is that there is no mention of virtues." This, he noted, is especially curious because the Catholic Church has for centuries talked about the good, or virtuous, life of individuals and societies. "If the Catholic bishops find it so hard to talk about virtue in public, it is not surprising that others find it nearly impossible." At least one other participant observed in this regard that maybe the reason the bishops didn't speak to "public virtues" is that they might have been understood to be suggesting that, as societies, the United States and the Soviet Union are not on a moral plane. That is to say, if the bishops had addressed the question of public virtue, they might have been read as implying that the United States, as a society, is morally superior to the Soviet Union and, further, that this is a factor to be taken into account in pondering questions of war and peace. Such ideas are, needless to say, deemed to be outrageously chauvinistic by many Americans.

Returning to what he described as "the reign of relativism," Allan Carlson of The Rockford Institute indicated that a remedy might be found in something like a religious revival. Such a revival, he wanted it understood, would have to be more than "another religious awakening." Religion as such is an ambiguous phenomenon and can often bring with it elements of prejudice and intolerance that undermine the need for civic virtue. The revival that Carlson had in mind involves a culture-forming public religion that could create a climate in which "virtue would seem like a natural pursuit, not a peculiarly religious interest." On the other hand, he granted that unless there is a manifestly religious component, there is a real danger that virtue would be "defined along purely political or ideological lines." In that event, a revival of virtue would end up in further polarization and would make "agreement on consensual norms" almost impossible.

By this point, Peter Berger was becoming impatient with the discussion. "As a sociologist," he thought the participants in the discussion were ignoring "the observable world out there." Was not Billington, for example, putting too much emphasis upon the university as the institution that should foster virtue? Why not focus on the police, or the army, or the courts, or a host of other institutions? Berger wanted to "concretize" the discussion and move away from the improbable assumption that "the average bus driver in Boston looks to the professors at Harvard for moral guidance." It was conceded that Berger might be right about where people actually get their notions of virtue, but it was nonetheless held to be important to take into account, as Nuechterlein had urged, the way in which the university tries to discredit those sources of virtue.

Joel Fleishman of Duke University asserted that much that was being said about the university did not square with his own experience. "I don't recognize an anti-virtue orthodoxy among the faculty at Duke, and I doubt if Duke is that different." There is, Fleishman said, a lively, if confused, interest in values, ethics, morality, virtue, and the like. He related what had happened at Duke some while back when he gave a public lecture calling for a resurgence of traditional values and a consensus on the normatively ethical. He had prepared his lecture with considerable trepidation, fearing that some would dismiss his argument as reactionary, and he was therefore all the more surprised by the overwhelmingly positive response. Perhaps, he suggested, Billington and others were being excessively dour about the current state of higher education. It just might be that there is an element of the self-fulfilling in such "pessimism."

Michael Novak, resident scholar at the American Enterprise Institute, entered the opening created by Fleishman. His intention was not to balance the discussion with a dose of optimism, he said, but he did think the group was overlooking some positive developments in the idea of virtue in American life. True, American society does tend toward a vulgar pragmatism, the absolutism of tolerance, and the divorce of private virtue from public life, but that is not the whole story, according to Novak. These tendencies make up a "short list of the vices of democratic capitalism," but the more important news is what Tocqueville saw happening generations ago. There is a new idea of virtue in American life and its cornerstone is "self-interest rightly understood." Admittedly, the virtues that stem from this notion are not of the heroic type. They are "the virtues of the middle range that point to the ideals that guide the lives of millions of ordinary people." Community spirit, hard work, and frugality are among the middle-range virtues he had in mind. "At least every four years both the Republican and Democratic parties try to claim these virtues as their own, and that's because they're so very American." Democratic capitalism does not often produce heroism, Novak acknowledged, but then heroism is by definition always in short supply. Its rarity cannot reasonably be blamed on "the system."

Stanley Hauerwas, also of Duke, had substantive objections to the course of the discussion, especially to some of Billington's initial arguments. What Hauerwas calls "the virtue tradition" sets him on a different path from "sermonizing about freedom without responsibility." As Aristotle saw it (and as Hauerwas sees it), virtue has much more to do with training than with freedom. "Becoming virtuous requires long training, as it is an esoteric achievement not accomplished by many. In particular, it requires apprenticeship to a master who can initiate another into the painful process of becoming a person of character—that is, someone capable of becoming virtuous."

According to Hauerwas, the emphasis on freedom frequently gets in the way of understanding virtue. "Many 'neoconservatives' are caught in this bind. They want society to recover 'traditional values,' which they rather uncritically identify with virtues, yet they adhere to an ideology that undercuts the very values to which they adhere. That is, they want a society that makes freedom of the individual the supreme value, but then they are upset when some use that freedom to buy pornography, and then they fall back into sermonizing about 'freedom without responsibility.' " In any event, Hauerwas indicated that he is not all that enamored of "the traditional values" that people say they want to get back to. Traditional morality, for example, has always been too ready to permit and even encourage acts of violence. Yesterday's morality needs to be critically reexamined, not uncritically invoked.

Hauerwas had yet another point. He was not so sure that Billington should scorn the contemporary interest in art as virtue. "The aesthetic is an essential component in the traditional understanding of the development of virtue," he argued. Great art trains the affections, teaches the meaning of beauty and the good, and creates "people of judgment." "Great art," said Hauerwas, "un-selfs the self, while bad art takes the self into ever deeper pools of narcissism." He agreed with Billington that art is not an acceptable substitute for morality, but he stressed that there is a connection between the two that needs to be appreciated more fully.

At the end of this first session, James Billington did not attempt to respond to all the points that had been made. Instead he focused on what he perceives to be the moral sense that is surprisingly vibrant in the American middle class, among millions of ordinary people who tend to be "invisible" in discussions such as this. "Key to our cultural problem is that this 'silent majority' is silent because it lacks a moral vocabulary for speaking in public." He suggested that helping to supply such a vocabulary should be a priority for people concerned about virtue, "or else the task will be taken over and monopolized by moral majoritarianism." It was evident that nobody in the room thought that a happy prospect.

VIRTUE AND DEMOCRACY

Opening the second session, Bernard Semmel expanded on his argument that religion (especially the Wesleyan revival in England and America) gave shape and force to our ideas about virtue and democracy. The passions for liberty, equality, and fraternity have been both powered and tempered by religious faith. We might do well to look for a renewal of virtue in the religious revival that is already underway in American life, then, Semmel suggested.

At this point, Peter Berger confessed to a doubt that had been nagging at him all day. Were we not talking altogether too vaguely about "a general virtue" and about "the virtues," which presumably are something more specific, he asked. It seemed to him that a definition of terms was called for. In response, Hauerwas volunteered a working definition of the virtues: "those powers that provide dispositions for acquiring the excellences that are appropriate for being human." Berger indicated that he was still not satisfied. Novak also protested that *dispositions* was the wrong word: "It sounds as though we are just talking about feelings." He suggested that virtues are similar to such everyday skills as driving a car and riding a bicycle. "They are things that can be done without conscious thought, by habit." Novak also insisted that the "excellences" sought must be freely chosen by virtuous persons.

Gilbert Meilaender of Oberlin was also worried that Hauerwas's definition might undermine the importance of "agency." The virtuous person is an active agent, he insisted, not merely a passive receiver of excellences defined by a tradition. Concurring with Meilaender, Robert Payton of the Exxon Education Foundation asserted that the importance of agency is also biblical. "In the parable of the rich young man," Payton noted, "the young man *chose* not to abide by Jesus' command to sell all that he owned." As the discussion took a turn toward definitions and even the Bible, Frank Alexander of Emory University's School of Law thought it necessary to point out a problem with Hauerwas's reference to "being human."

We cannot assume, said Alexander, that we mean the same thing by "being human" that, for example, Aristotle meant. From a Christian perspective there are two truths to be asserted about "being human": there is the fact that we have been created in the image of God, but there is also the fact of our fallen or corrupted nature. Alexander suggested that Hauerwas was neglecting the latter reality. Eric Lincoln disagreed, but he also objected to Hauerwas's definition because it is too cumbersome. A good working definition of virtue, in Lincoln's view, is that "virtue is the disposition to behave responsibly, and vice the disposition to behave irresponsibly." At this point Richard Neuhaus stepped out of his role as moderator to express satisfaction that vice had finally been mentioned. He suggested that it might be easier to get a consensus on vice than on virtue, and if so, then virtue might be defined as the opposite of vice and virtuous behavior as the opposite of vicious behavior. After further definitional wrangling, there was general agreement that it is probably reflective of our "cultural crisis" that half-way through a conference on virtue there was no certain agreement on what is meant by virtue.

John Barbour of Saint Olaf College reminded the group that however virtues are defined, it is agreed that they are historically transmitted. "Virtues require real, living communities in which people grow up with stories of virtue, especially of heroic virtue," he noted. A crucial question, as he sees it, is whether there are heroic stories capable of schooling the national community in virtue. Billington responded that our stock of stories has been sharply diminished. "The 1960s did a demolition job on our national stories, not just by debunking one after another, but, much more devastatingly, by disseminating the idea that individuals don't matter that much, that individual behavior is determined by forces beyond the control of the individual." According to Billington, it is now obvious that even the biblical stories are no longer lodged in the national memory. At the same time, he remains hopeful that there is still a lively idea that something like the "power of example" should be preserved, and that that idea, which is most deeply grounded in religion, is waiting to be rediscovered and reasserted in American life.

Margaret Steinfels cautioned the group that heroism is a sometime thing: "You can't say that there aren't heroes and heroines in American life. The popular culture is throwing them up all the time, but they come and go; they're often no more than fads." Expressing agreement, Allan Carlson came up with a short "all-star list" of popular heroes: Michael Jackson, John Wayne, Clint Eastwood, Luke Skywalker. He suggested that we should not dismiss such a list out of hand: "Whether or not they are in fact exemplary characters, they do point to a popular yearning for heroes and heroic stories."

James Nuechterlein agreed that our culture is not bereft of heroes, but he suggested that we are confused about the ways in which some of them represent private virtues and others public virtues, and about what connection, if any, there is between private and public virtue. Admitting that he was citing an extreme example, he asked whether it was not possible that some people would view Barry Goldwater as being exemplary for his private virtue while Lyndon Johnson's public virtue would be held up for emulation? James Hitchcock of St. Louis University was skeptical. He suggested that "the high modernist agenda" has been largely successful in discrediting the idea of virtue itself in our culture. Even such partisan heroisms as Nuechterlein thinks possible are depressingly superficial, he indicated. According to Hitchcock, we may cheer on some people rather than others, but few people take seriously the notion that the reason for cheering is that such individuals represent moral absolutes that make a demand upon us. Novak, once again risking optimism, urged the conference not to overlook the everyday function of sports, games, and contests in teaching virtue. Even popular outrage at the "corruption" of professional sports, he indicated, shows that most Americans believe these sports should exemplify values that are properly described as virtuous. And thus the idea emerged again that virtue might be illumined by the shadow of vice.

But the discussion had now been turned to the distinction between private and public virtue. There was no ready consensus that the distinction is valid. Michael Novak argued that it is not only valid but essential. "Of course a person who is virtuous in private life can act viciously in public affairs," he asserted, citing the instance of a military officer who has an exemplary family life, is highly skilled and disciplined, and yet obeys orders to murder the innocent. "Surely modern history has given us ample examples of this dichotomy between private and public virtue," he said. Similarly, he pointed out, there are numerous examples of virtuous persons who end up doing well-intentioned but horrible things in the public sphere because they lack such public virtues as political prudence.

The distinction between private and public virtue received the strongest challenge from Hauerwas. "The idea that there is private or personal virtue and then there is public or political virtue is utterly corrupting," he stated. It is an idea that many people learned from Reinhold Niebuhr, he said, and it is urgent that it be unlearned. Niebuhr taught that "procedural democracy" could produce a just society without just citizens, but Hauerwas finds this entirely unconvincing. The distinction between private and public virtue is, said Hauerwas, alien to the "virtue tradition" he would advance and is "vicious" in its consequences:

> This is a modern and debilitating distinction. In the past it was assumed that a person of virtue, even if not directly involved in politics, served a political function. The person of integrity is a political resource; his character makes possible a society that would otherwise be impossible. When we can't count on the other person to be virtuous, we must then rely on institutions, most often the state, to rectify our inability to trust someone to be virtuous. The more we rely on the state to sustain the relations necessary for social life, the less it seems we need people of virtue—and that's how the whole vicious cycle begins.

According to Hauerwas, the person of virtue in public life is the person who is capable of disinterestedness, and therefore capable of doing justice. Hauerwas does not deny that involvement in the political realm may mean getting "dirty hands," but it is only the virtuous person who can recognize that moral ambiguity and who will refuse to excuse it by saying "that's politics." The alternative is to say that the political inevitably corrupts the person of virtue, and the result of this is to abandon politics to a cynicism that reduces the political to nothing more than a struggle for power.

Rockne McCarthy of Dordt College was sympathetic to Hauerwas's argument, but he contended that it places too much emphasis on the role of the state. "Public" does not mean only, or even mainly, the state, he insisted. Other institutions have public roles—churches, synagogues, private schools, corporations. In a democratic society, these "mediating structures" not only transmit the traditions of virtue but also, along with the state, help to regulate the consequences when individuals do not behave virtuously. The somewhat tentative result of these exchanges seemed to be an agreement with Hauerwas that the virtuous person strives to act virtuously in all circumstances, private and public. However, there was also agreement with Novak and others that some acts we might deem virtuous in public behavior we would not deem virtuous in private behavior. It was suggested, for example, that we would expect a female judge to deal impartially with those brought before the bench, but if, in her role as a mother, she showed no partiality toward her own children, we would have a quite different judgment. But some argued this is not an example of private as distinct from public virtues but rather an example of a single set of virtues that calls for diverse actions in diverse situations. If that is so, it may be that we ought not to speculate about private and public virtues but rather begin to develop a unified understanding of the virtues to be appropriately acted upon in various circumstances. And, of course, to know what is appropriate requires one of the four "cardinal virtues," namely prudence.

But are we not deceiving ourselves by thinking that we will advance virtue by clarifying what it means, asked James Hitchcock. In a society such as ours, the very idea of virtue—no matter how poorly conceived—is odious to what is probably a growing number of people. The democratic impulse, as it is presently at work, is undermining the possibility of virtue:

> Through most of American history there was little evident trouble positing political equality on the one hand and some sense of moral hierarchy on the other. Increasingly, however, equality within the democratic system is understood to mean that all people are equal in the sense that no person can claim to be better than another in any way. Thus the very term "virtue" raises hackles, implying as it does that it is a quality that some possess and others do not, or some possess more than others.

Rockne McCarthy acknowledged that he could not disprove Hitchcock's doleful view of democracy's future, but he argued that hope lies in making America more democratic rather than less. "If we understand politics as a moral enterprise, then the goal must be to open up the political system to engage those who have been excluded or marginalized," he suggested. Semmel returned to his point that a religious resurgence can do again what it once did for the revitalization of democratic governance. Steinfels said she did not want to throw cold water on the democratic prospect, but she was profoundly skeptical. "It is very difficult, it is not at all clear, that the enthusiasm of religious communities can be translated into the virtue of society at large, or even that those enthusiasms would be good for society," she said. Whether or not such a translation is possible, and whether or not it would be good for democracy, Hauerwas indicated that he wants no part of it. This, he said, is the "functionalist" approach to religion—"Convert more people to make society more virtuous"—and it constitutes a debasement of religion. "Reli-

gious people are what they are and do what they do not because
it is a public benefit but because of the truth that gathers and
guides their religious communities," Hauerwas insisted. He did
not deny that religion might play an important role, even a
critical role, in reconstructing democratic virtue, but religion
that is deliberately used as an end to public virtue is a poor excuse
for religion. "True religion ain't for hire."

The thought had cropped up several times that there is a
certain tension between "the virtue tradition" and the democratic idea. Talk about virtue assumes excellences that are traditional, definite, in place. Democracy seems not only to entail a
"leveling" of the qualities we call virtues but also to suggest that
they are inherently tentative, experimental, and open-ended. Is
it worth discussing, Neuhaus inquired, the "virtue of democracy
itself"? That is to say, short of the coming of the Kingdom, is the
democratic idea essential to keeping society open for the debate
about the good, the virtuous?

Jean Bethke Elshtain of the University of Massachusetts
suggested that this open-endedness is indeed necessary. "The
meaning of such high-voltage words as *equality* is contested, must
be contested. The same way with *justice* or *freedom*. We can
never hope for, we should never want, a final cloture to debates
as to what such words mean or the range of their application. Of
course our ideas, our visions of the just and free society will differ;
that is the stuff of political debate. It is a democratic virtue that
is to be nurtured. To cut it off is the death of politics."

At this point Neuhaus quite shamelessly abandoned the
moderator's part to affirm the point being made by Elshtain and
others. He argued that the cultivation of an ever more inclusive
debate is essential to democratic virtue. Persons and institutions
take part in the give and take not necessarily for the sake of
democracy itself but for the sake of the truth for which they
contend. The virtue of this democratic exchange is that it calls
forth other virtues—honesty, humility, competence, compro-
mise, toleration, patience, and the like. This understanding of
democracy, Neuhaus noted, is consonant with the analysis of
A. D. Lindsay, who traces the emergence of democratic governance from English Puritanism. But today genuine democracy in
America is inhibited by an elite that assumes either that there is
no truth or that whatever truth does exist is purely subjective and
therefore not fit subject for public debate. Because of these elite

assumptions, true democratic debate over the good is avoided. "Democratic exchange is replaced by the politics of evasion. Government senses the decline of the public debate and, discerning the moral vacuum that is thus created, assumes an ever larger and more assertive role. Silence replaces democratic debate, and then regulation—the noise of the shuffling of government forms— replaces the silence."

Hauerwas declared himself somewhat skeptical of this vaunted freedom of democratic exchange. There is also the very real danger of "totalitarian freedom," said he. This was greeted with raised eyebrows and some vocal protest from around the room. James Billington in particular indicated his annoyance with "Orwellian twists" that end up defining freedom as slavery. Hauerwas hastened to retrieve the moment by arguing that the modern phenomenon of totalitarianism can thrive only where people are uprooted from their particular loyalties and "stories." When that happens, the "storyless masses" are herded into the colosseum and the "story" of the state is forced upon them. Liberal democratic societies can also, in a more subtle and benevolent way, undermine the loyalties and stories of their people. The result is that citizens of a democracy become vulnerable to the manipulative whims of powerful institutions, including the government. Hauerwas was not suggesting that America is a totalitarian society; "I am saying that we are the mirror image of the Soviet Union. These are the two great Enlightenment societies."

Michael Novak, among others, found these assertions entirely unacceptable. First, he said, as a matter of historical fact, totalitarianism did not come by way of Enlightenment individualism. Russia, China, Cuba, and other totalitarian societies did not see themselves, and in fact were not, following the path of the Enlightenment. Second, the Soviet Union is hardly a "mirror image" of the United States. Admittedly, America is not the Kingdom of God on earth. No nation is. But can it be doubted that it is morally superior to the Soviet Union? Just for starters, the American government has not routinely murdered millions of its own citizens. Contra Hauerwas, freedom is a virtue and, at least to a remarkable extent, it has been instrumental in the cultivation of other democratic virtues.

Hauerwas clarified his point:

In matters of foreign policy the virtues of liberal society are thought by some people to legitimize anything we must do to oppose the Soviet Union. Yet at the same time, those very virtues have an acid effect on the very values that legitimize the condemnation of the Soviets. I do not doubt that it is a fearful thing to live in a totalitarian regime, but it at least seems a matter of honesty that the very criticisms that the "neoconservatives" make against our society's moral laxity should temper somewhat their enthusiasm for the righteousness of America. No doubt the leaders of the Soviet Union have killed millions of their own people, but it is also true that millions have been killed in America, not by our government, but by people exercising their freedom of choice.

On this note of democratic debate the second session ended. Bernard Semmel had opened it by underscoring the role of religion in nurturing the virtues of democratic society. The third session was to turn more specifically to the place of virtue in contemporary religious thought, but it ended up more a discussion of pornography than of piety—or, as may in fact be the case, the connection between the two.

PIETY AND PORNOGRAPHY

Expanding upon his paper, Gilbert Meilaender asked what kinds of communities can nurture and transmit virtues in a free society. His answer was somewhat ironic: communities that are serious about ethical behavior cannot be entirely "democratic" in the conventional meaning of that term. That is to say, churches, schools, families, and the like, cannot be absolutely pluralistic and open if they are in fact serious about transmitting virtues. If they were to be entirely open, they would simply reflect the dominant values in the general culture. If they adopt a simplistic policy of "live and let live," what makes them distinctive would surely die.

That said, Meilaender proceeded to argue that communities that are serious about virtues cannot be absolutely structured, rigid, and sealed off from the general culture either. They cannot be dictatorships, not even benevolent dictatorships. On the one hand is the you-pay-your-money-and-you-take-your-choice style of liberalism; on the other hand is tribalism or mini-totalitarianism. Communities of virtue must set boundaries or they are not communities in a very significant sense. But they must also allow for a measured degree of freedom and openness—not because they doubt their own values, but because they recognize that the "vocation to virtue" cannot be fulfilled in isolation. While they take to heart the commandments of virtue, those very commandments lead them to the prayer of confession. They are forever open to receive the gift of grace that alone helps them to respond, however imperfectly, to the call to virtue. For communities of virtue, there is a necessary tension between freedom and the standards they affirm. Such a tension cannot be resolved, but it can be survived. More than that, it must be lived through, and can only be lived through by the gift of grace. (Meilaender noted that he is, not so incidentally, a Christian of the Lutheran persuasion.)

Since Peter Berger had taken over the chair, Neuhaus felt free to join in the debate, and he returned to the idea of "the virtue of democracy." It is precisely a virtue of liberal democracy, he said, that it acknowledges and permits the unresolvability of some social tensions, especially where "prepolitical truths" come into conflict. That is, liberal democracy is not designed to resolve, and should not be asked to resolve, "first-principle questions." In support of this point, Neuhaus cited the tortuous difficulties posed by the abortion debate's question of who belongs to the human community for which we accept societal responsibility. The liberal democratic idea also recognizes, said Neuhaus, the important part that contingency plays in history; it does not assume that everything is subject to political design. There is in liberal democracy, at least as Neuhaus would propound it, a humility that is akin to the sense of grace that Meilaender affirms. Joel Fleishman pointed out that this is not just a matter of attitude; it has an institutional entailment: liberal democracy "gives space" to the witness and operation of other institutions, such as religion. One problem today, said Fleishman, is that the religious communities are not sufficiently aware of "democracy's gift of public space," and therefore they tend to withhold their moral support from the democratic idea.

In light of this praise for liberal democracy, Charles Glenn of the Massachusetts Department of Education's Bureau of Equal Educational Opportunity felt called upon to offer a cautionary word. For all its merits, said Glenn, we should not forget that liberal societies also tend to have a profoundly "acid effect" on communities of virtue. In free societies, communities of virtue experience an erosion of their standards over time, an expansion of unprincipled freedom, a decay in their cohesiveness. Peter Berger confesses that being moderator made him feel like "a muzzled ox" and announced that he was removing the muzzle. "I have no idea what we're talking about," he said. "I suggest that we concretize this discussion by focusing on one empirically available area of human life." The conference was open to the suggestion and elected the issue of pornography.

Jean Elshtain opened the discussion by arguing that the current debate about pornography is grossly oversimplified and reflects our inability to talk about virtue in public. On the one side is the American Civil Liberties Union and on the other the moral majoritarians. The one side gives the seller and buyer of pornography absolute and unrestricted liberty while the other speaks again and again about censorship. In the terms posed, the debate is deadlocked. Given the current state of law on pornography, the ACLU almost always wins the specific cases. There is deep uneasiness about this in our society (not only among moral majoritarians), but there are few ideas about how the debate can be restructured in a way that breaks the present impasse.

At this point some urged that we pause and explore the empirical reality of pornography in American life. Is it that much different from what had gone on before? Neuhaus suggested that it is, and invoked Chesterton's observation that "all morality is finally a matter of drawing lines." He contended that the lines are obviously being drawn today at places quite different from where they were, say, thirty years ago. Then it was unself-consciously stated that a "sense of decency" prevailed on one side of the line. On the other side of the line was what was recognized as vicious or obscene. One can empirically point to the redrawing of lines in a series of specifiable decisions made by specifiable people. What used to be called "girlie magazines" went from partial nudity to exposing all. Publications of a certain genre were taken from under the counter and are now prominently displayed next to the toothpaste. The "sense of decency" has been disestablished in law and popular behavior as it had earlier been disdained among some of the cultural elite. One can argue whether this change is for better or worse, but there is no doubt that there has been dramatic and empirically verifiable change.

James Hitchcock stated his belief that the change is emphatically for the worse and that it is inherent in the "demythologizing" bias of the modern mindset. There is a compulsive need to shatter taboos, he said, which stems from an unprincipled idea of freedom—namely, that one must not only have but must also act upon the freedom to do anything. Hauerwas did not challenge Hitchcock's point, but he did suggest that there is a more "institutionally specific" side of the question. The institution he had in mind was marriage. "I came to understand the vice of pornography from the virtue of marriage," he said. In the Judeo-Christian tradition, sex is intended for the intimacy of monogamous marriage, and that ideal is protected by a community of virtue, such as the church. Pornography is wrong because it destroys intimacy and makes sex common.

James Billington suggested that "making sex common" also has political ramifications. A distinguished historian of modern revolutions, Billington reported that in his research he has been surprised to discover how many revolutionaries were, at some point in their careers, pornographers or proponents of pornography. No fewer than five of the key leaders of the French Revolution, for example, had been professional pornographers before becoming professional revolutionaries. This does not mean, he hastened to add, that there is a necessary or causal connection between pornography and violent revolution, but it is not farfetched to speculate that there is a relationship between assaulting the traditional structuring of sexual behavior and assaulting "the old order at its heart."

James Nuechterlein expressed his puzzlement at the reluctance of the churches to respond to the cultural attack against monogamous marriage. In his experience, the churches are remarkably reticent on such issues as chastity and fidelity. He had recently heard a pastor address these subjects in a forthright manner in a sermon but afterward a friend had remarked, "There the church goes again, always harping on sex." What struck Nuechterlein as odd about this is that he could not remember having heard a similar sermon for at least ten years—and neither, when pressed, could his friend. Nuechterlein speculated that perhaps the churches are silent about marriage and sex precisely because they are intimidated by a widely disseminated cultural stereotype that the churches are "obsessed" by the subject.

Margaret Steinfels intervened to object that the conference

was being entirely too narrow in its "working idea of pornography." Sure, pornography is found in sleazy bookstores, but it is also in Madison Avenue advertising. Advertising's suggestive photography and prose are nothing but thinly veiled "soft porn." Is it the case that our kind of economic system makes such pornography an essential ingredient in doing business?

Michael Novak noted that he had already looked into that question and come up with some considered answers. He suggested that the conferees were being excessively negative in their assessment of pornography in American life, especially in attributing it to "the system." He professed himself to be astonished at the large numbers of people in our society who are chaste in singleness and faithful in marriage. We should not, he said, be taken in by the media's favorite pastime of pretending to shock the bourgeoisie. The media always scramble to dwell on the newest perversity, but this has only a limited effect on what people actually do in their lives. In any case, said Novak, we should not overlook the pervasiveness of sin. We are dealing, in this or any society, with human beings, with sinners. In specific response to Steinfels, Novak suggested that the prevalence of pornography indicates little or nothing about "the system" but a great deal about those who work in the system. As he himself has pointed out to business leaders, they frequently do employ advertising that undercuts the moral foundations of bourgeois culture. When they undercut virtues such as discipline, fidelity, and sacrifice, they are hurting themselves and the economic system they claim to champion.

As to what is to be done about the problems signaled by pornography, there was little agreement. Robert Payton argued that we, as a society, are inculcating at a very early age the assumptions on which pornography flourishes. He is not opposed to "sex education" of the right kind in the schools, but he noted that what presently passes for sex education seems to be correlated with increased sexual activity of the kind that invites pornographic exploitation. The specific problem is that little connection is made in such courses between sexuality and virtue. Robert Rodes added that it is these societal assumptions that need to be addressed, that pornography can be addressed in only a very limited way by law. "Liberal democracy is more form than content, more procedure than philosophy," said Rodes. "The content and philosophy, if there is to be such, must be supplied by the participants in the democratic society." In his view, the procedural adjustments that are possible are so minor as to be almost beside the point.

What is needed is more public assertiveness on the part of "communities of virtue," said Allan Carlson. But it is a new circumstance that these communities of virtue now feel themselves opposed by the general culture. Not long ago, said Carlson, there was in America a rather pervasive notion that there is such a thing as an "American character," integrating a distinct set of virtues; he cited Dean Rusk and Walt Rostow as individuals who exemplified it. But that notion is very near to being dead now. Admittedly, it was very "WASPish" and had other limitations, but it did assume a life based upon a philosophy in which "the virtues" were key.

Hauerwas expressed some skepticism about the possibility of reconstituting such a public or generalized idea of virtues. He maintained that whatever hope there is rests with communities of virtue such as the churches, or such as the churches ought to be. This does not mean withdrawal from concern for the public, he said, but it does mean the churches make their most important contribution by challenging the assumptions of the culture. "For example, one of the greatest things the churches could do for our culture is to challenge the myth of sexual repression," he stated. The churches must ask themselves what kind of society we have to be "in order to maintain singles in celibacy and husbands and wives in faithfulness." Then the churches should strive to be that kind of society, in the hope that the larger society will take note of the genuinely liberating possibility that the churches exemplify.

The question of whether the churches ought to be that kind of exemplary community "over against" the larger society raises the old distinction between "sect" and "church." Speaking as a Roman Catholic, Brian Benestad noted the sect/church distinction can be overdone. The Roman Catholic Church, which is presumably the archetype of the "church" model, has traditionally understood that part of its public vocation is to be somewhat different from the generalized world of "the public." The Catholic Church sees itself as "leaven" in the society and addresses its social teachings both to the society at large and to the members of the Catholic community. Benestad readily acknowledges that the Catholic Church, like other churches, has never quite got the hang of doing this either consistently or with maximum effect. Especially on questions of sexuality this double task has been difficult, given the libertine directions of American culture.

Neuhaus said that the churches should be more assertive and unapologetic when it comes to shaping the general culture. "Of course people will say, 'You're trying to impose your values on the rest of us,' but we shouldn't be intimidated by that," he insisted. There is nothing undemocratic about trying to persuade people of the truth of what you believe to be true. "This does not violate pluralism. Pluralism is civil contestation on matters of great moment. What most people call pluralism today is really a monism of evasion in the name of tolerance." But Joel Fleishman questioned whether Neuhaus's approach doesn't entail drawing new and quite distinct lines. Yes, responded Neuhaus, lines should be drawn at some points. We should say, for instance, that such things as incest, sadomasochistic theater involving severe bodily injury or death, and the like are simply unthinkable and therefore outlawed—that is, outside what is countenanced by law.

John Barbour was not unsympathetic to this approach, but he offered the caution that churches must remember they don't have all the answers for society. They have things to learn from the society, even while they attempt to instruct. Churches should, said Barbour, develop "styles appropriate to public witness," which means they should distance themselves from self-righteousness and the denunciatory posture that marks some religious witness in the public square. Here Gilbert Meilaender expanded on a point he made in his paper—that wisdom about virtue involves a note of the "felicitous." The churches and other communities of virtue do not "possess a moral superiority" so much as they witness to the gift-like character of the good. In this way they keep themselves open, and help other institutions to be open, to the God who has called them into existence. In sum, said Meilaender, communities of virtue must acknowledge that their understanding of virtue is alien to the culture while, at the same time, they try to appeal to the best aspirations within the culture. "Sect" and "church" are both essential to the transformation of culture, but no matter how successful that transformation may be, the culture will always remain "alien" in the sense of being far short of the eschatological community of virtue to which the church witnesses.

THE LAW AS VIRTUOUS ASPIRATION

Robert Rodes made the point that there is great confusion about what the law should and should not do, can and cannot do. Conventional "conservative" and "liberal" attitudes to the contrary notwithstanding, law should do more than throw vicious criminals into jail or absolutize freedom, he argued; it should do no less than attempt to guide society toward the virtues. "Society should provide the conditions, including laws, under which people can be perfected in virtue, insofar as that is possible," he said. The realm of law includes many facets—rewards, punishments, regulations, the dissemination of information—all of which should be enlisted in nudging citizens toward virtue.

For this to happen, the virtues must rest upon a "philosophical consensus" in a society. To a degree the churches, as "signs and safeguards of the transcendence of the person," assist the society in reaching that consensus. Unfortunately, said Rodes, the legal system today has turned away from and implicitly denies the existence of a moral consensus. For instance, on many of what people perceive to be "moral issues," the law primarily serves to protect the professions and their decision-making prerogatives. A professional librarian can permanently remove a book from the school library, for instance, but a school board acting upon a societal consensus would immediately be embroiled in a legal battle over "censorship" if it did the same thing. Citing this and other examples, Rodes argued for a restoration of the understanding that law has to do with society's "moral aspirations."

This view of the law was politely but pointedly challenged by Frank Alexander as being "overly idealized." Rodes's idea of law is full of good intentions, he said, but behind the good intentions hide some destructive tendencies. One such tendency is majoritarianism; another is cynicism: the desire to accomplish so much by means of the law inevitably ends in "either bitter success or bitter failure." The success embitters those who dissent from the triumphant morality, and the failure embitters those who champion the morality. "Law is a blunt instrument," said Alexander, "and should be wielded with extreme caution." A better way to think about the purpose of the law, he urged, is to view it as making room for others to bear witness. This has the additional, and not inconsiderable, virtue of keeping the law

limited. "And keeping the government limited," added Nuechterlein in agreement.

Everett Ladd of the University of Connecticut's Roper
Center expressed a somewhat more sanguine view of the law, or
at least of the courts, today. Admittedly, judges do not all share
a single view of virtue, but neither are they as indifferent to
virtue as some people suggest. Ladd pointed to the role of the
courts in civil rights reform over the past several decades, suggesting that this illustrates the readiness of American law to
address questions of moral right and wrong. Peter Berger urged
that the conference was in danger of "sacralizing" law. "There
is," he said, "a halo effect surrounding American law. Laws are
turned into 'the law,' and black-robed justices are treated as priests
who presumably discern the 'voice of the gods.'" The result,
according to Berger, is that judges believe they have the authority, even the obligation, to pontificate on everything under the
sun   even the question of when human life begins. Berger asserted that the halo needs to be knocked off, that the law needs
to be "secularized" and "demythologized."

James Hitchcock added to Berger's views:

> The "imperial judiciary" is now the closest thing to a high
> priesthood which America has. But the rise of the judiciary
> is not due primarily to the judge's lust for power, nor even
> to the revolution in constitutional thought which has oc-
> curred since the time of the New Deal. Rather the judiciary
> now merely moves to fill the moral vacuum which has been
> created at the heart of the society. Even in a society whose
> members are officially moral agnostics, practical decisions
> must be constantly made which imply moral beliefs. The
> courts now increasingly make those decisions, usually offering
> what purport to be compelling moral arguments.

Frank Alexander quoted a judge of the Philadelphia Court of
Common Pleas who said, "I feel like a black-robed priest performing the last rites of a dying faith." If this is not a case of the
cynicism he mentioned earlier, Alexander noted, it is dangerous-
ly close to it.

Robert Payton picked up on the earlier observation that the
law creates space for other institutions to bear witness. One of
those often-overlooked institutions, he said, is philanthropy: "Although the philanthropic tradition has been neglected by intellectuals and ignored by the universities, it has been encouraged

to flourish by the legal system." The law protects philanthropy, and philanthropy provides the room (and, quite literally, the rooms, such as the one we occupied at the University Club) for people to bear witness. Private giving for public purposes, Payton noted, is ninety percent from individuals and ten percent from corporations and foundations. It is 85 million people performing voluntary services estimated to be worth $65 billion per year. The volunteer movements that eventually make their impact on public policy almost always begin with philanthropy. "Here is where the ideas and practice of the virtues are sustained in American life." said Payton. "The law is essential to the philanthropic tradition, but it is not so much an institution that embodies aspirations as a protection of institutions that exercise moral aspirations." He underscored the point that this is something peculiar to American life: "The way in which a conference such as this happens is completely foreign to European societies, for example."

To Payton's rather hopeful intervention Bernard Semmel responded with several concerns. He agreed with Payton about the importance of philanthropy but noted that his viewpoint is rare among social analysts today. What passes for analysis of American life in the high culture conventionally ignores the philanthropic dimension altogether, he suggested, or relegates it to the status of being something "vestigial" left over from "the good old days that never were." He wondered too whether it was not possible that Americans are becoming less generous in their charitable giving. Leading politicians seem unembarrassed by the piddling amounts they give to charity, he noted, and the women's movement "is conducting a crusade against voluntary service as a form of exploitation." However much the law may protect philanthropy, it will not be enough to sustain this dimension of American life, in Semmel's view.

Jean Elshtain wanted to go back to Rodes's argument about law and "moral consensus." She contended that the very idea of a moral consensus is undercut today by both deliberate argumentation and habits of speech. "There is an intellectual bias against some ideals, maybe against ideals as such," Elshtain said, as is evident in connection with the "nuclear family." There is an intense intellectual focus on the twisted social problems of the nuclear family—wife beating, incest, and on and on. There has been an implicit shift in the argumentation away from focusing on the perversions of the family to focusing on the family as a perversion. This is a process of "deconstruction" that has been aimed not only at the family but also at other "virtue-possessing and virtue-transmitting institutions," she argued. All of this contributes to an erosion of moral consensus, as do habits of speech favored by "specialists." We live in a society of "human resource managers," "social service providers," and "clients." When we begin to think of ourselves in this jargon, the classical definitions of citizenship and politics become almost impossible. Tying into Rodes's earlier point, Elshtain noted that the law increasingly reinforces the "professionalization" that militates against moral consensus, or even moral discourse.

James Hitchcock suggested that the absence of moral consensus is reflected in the growing litigiousness of the American people. Of course, he added, that growth is not unaffected by the greed of the ever-expanding ranks of lawyers. Lawyers have a deep stake in taking issues to court that might be settled out of court if people were still able to talk with one another about rights and wrongs. Allan Carlson proposed that survey research, such as that done by Daniel Yankelovich, indicates that there may be several moral "consensuses" among Americans. About twenty percent of the population professes, and perhaps practices, what might be called Puritan virtues. That is to say they are comfortable with traditional, middle-class, bourgeois values. Another twenty percent is "into the self." Their prized virtues are self-esteem, self-improvement, self-cultivation, self-realization, and the like. The remaining sixty percent is of a split mind—sometimes bourgeois, sometimes anti-bourgeois. "The result is a values Balkanization," Carlson concluded, "and this makes one moral consensus almost impossible."

The conference was clearly moving away from Rodes's confidence in "law as aspiration" and its connection with moral consensus. James Billington elaborated on Carlson's misgivings, suggesting that our society seems to be breeding two elite classes: "the literate elite and the numerate elite." The first lives by words, the second by numbers. "Young hot-shot lawyers epitomize the first elite; young hot-shot bankers and investors the latter," said Billington. In private life both groups subscribe to a "liberated lifestyle" which is presumably conducive to a "liberated self." Neither has the slightest interest in what we were describing as a moral or philosophical consensus for the society.

Billington noted that some people thought the election of Ronald Reagan would contribute to such a consensus, but he said he for one didn't believe this had happened. Like its predecessors, the Reagan administration seems content to build "a Versailles culture on the Potomac." The most glaring illustration of "values Balkanization," he said, is the way in which public schools are permitted to drift aimlessly on a "value-free" sea, or at best on a sea of questionable values. Charles Glenn agreed, describing how, in hundreds of meetings with public school educators, "I almost never have heard any mention of religion or faith or character or virtue." He added that it is not that educators are not concerned about these questions; it is rather that they simply don't know how to raise such questions in public. He indicated that this reveals an absence of philosophical consensus that law can do little to remedy.

These may be the sobering realities, Neuhaus remarked, but is there not at least a semblance of consensus in the way people talk about "social justice"? People have conflicting notions about what it means in particulars, but almost all are agreed that social justice is a very good thing in general. It didn't take long to become apparent that even in this room there is little agreement on whether "social justice" is a term with any usable content. Benestad observed that the term "social justice" first appeared in the nineteenth century in connection with philosophical reflection on natural law. In 1931 Pius used it in an encyclical. The history of the term, according to Benestad, connects with a Thomistic idea of legal justice, and that idea of legal justice, in turn, involves the pursuit of the virtues. "It was then assumed," Benestad said, "that the doing of justice depended on a virtuous agent, whereas today it is widely thought that 'social justice' can be done quite apart from the virtues." The significant turnaround consists in the fact that social justice has now come to mean "what other people owe me, not what I owe to the well-being of society." Amazingly enough, "participating in 'social justice work' today seems to excuse a person from the pursuit of a virtuous life, or, to put it differently, 'social justice work' is the virtue that makes up for the absence of the other virtues."

Hauerwas was at least equally suspicious of the invocation of "social justice." "The important question which a lot of 'social justice' talk obscures is the question of what kind of society encourages the development of just people," he said. Contemporary notions of social justice are premised upon "rights" and self-interest, whereas, according to Hauerwas, the "virtue tradition" asks first of all about the quality of the self that is interested. Elshtain remarked that the call for "social justice" frequently results in injustices, since it obscures what Nietzsche correctly perceived as the "will to power." Berger added that "social justice" is an "empty formula" into which politicians, theologians, and activists pour whatever meaning they wish. Having raised the question of "social justice" and therefore being responsible for having exposed it to such withering comment, Neuhaus felt obligated to put in a good word for the term. Expressions such as "social justice" or "a just society" have a limited validity, he suggested, in that social systems, while not in themselves just or unjust, do permit or encourage a greater or lesser degree of behavior that may properly be termed just or unjust.

This was cutting it too fine for Berger, who urged that "justice" is best defined by reference to "injustice." The term "justice" has no meaning, he said; "a consensus can more readily be established in recognizing the commission of injustices" (he confessed that he has an affinity for particularities and therefore thinks it more useful to refer to injustice in the plural). Reacting to Rodes's starting point, several conferees suggested that our understanding of law might best be framed negatively: it is more a matter of saying No to injustices than a matter of the positive cultivation of virtue. And this, they pointed out, is related to the broader argument made earlier, that virtues are illuminated by vices.

By the end of these two days of discussion, Peter Berger announced that he had been almost convinced that the term "virtue" is of very little use. At one point he said that he had resolved never to use the word again. Others—most vocally, Meilaender and Hauerwas—objected. They were not content to talk only about vice, evil, and injustice and then to let virtue emerge as the implicit opposite of these negatives. "Perhaps we cannot define justice very closely," said Meilaender, "but we know that there are actions appropriate to certain situations, and we recognize that action as good, and we call it just." He referred approvingly to Michael Walzer's notion of "spheres of justice" in which "the felicity of the right thing is done." Rockne McCarthy also insisted upon a "reciprocity" between definitions of virtue and vice, citing marriage and parenthood as "spheres" in which we recognize "brokenness" in light of "shalom," and "shalom" in the shadow of "brokenness."

In summing up, several people observed that, whether or not we can define it, the human being is a creature that has no choice but to talk about virtue, including the virtue of justice. If we did not speak about it, debate it, invoke it, the very stones would cry out in protest. To which Nuechterlein added that, in all our talking about virtue, we should not forget that every generation has been convinced that in its time virtue was in decline. Yes, several voices broke in, but that does not mean that virtue is not in decline in this generation. As someone has observed, paranoids too can be persecuted.

Alasdair MacIntyre's *After Virtue* was hardly mentioned at the conference, but it is safe to assume that its argument hovered over the meeting. In the concluding reflections of that book, MacIntyre writes that his thesis does not imply "a generalised social pessimism." And yet many believe that pessimism is precisely the right word to describe his suggestion that the best we can do now is to retreat to small communities of virtue. "What matters at this stage," MacIntyre tells us,

> is the construction of local forms of community within which civility and the intellectual and moral life can be sustained through the new dark ages which are already upon us. And if the tradition of the virtues was able to survive the horrors of the last dark ages, we are not entirely without grounds for hope. This time however the barbarians are not waiting beyond the frontiers; they have already been governing us for quite some time. And it is our lack of consciousness of this that constitutes part of our predicament. We are waiting not for a Godot, but for another— doubtless very different—St. Benedict.

The participants in the "Virtue—Public and Private" conference did not reach so doleful a verdict perhaps because, unlike MacIntyre, they were not dealing so exclusively with the history of ideas. The discussion was more attuned to the vitalities of virtue in the experience of everyday life. These vitalities are frequently weak and may well be vestigial, but the conferees seemed to agree that they are there to be nurtured. They did not dispute the importance of sect-like, even monastic-like, communities of virtue. Indeed, such communities keep the rumor of virtue alive in the larger society. Yet it is in that larger society also that the conferees detected what Meilaender called "felicity" and what many of us take to be evidence of the grace of God. It was not within the competence of this or any conference to determine whether that modestly hopeful conclusion is the result of faith or, as MacIntyre might have it, "lack of consciousness."

Participants

Frank S. Alexander
School of Law
Emory University

John D. Barbour
Department of Religion
St. Olaf College

Brian Benestad
Department of Theology and
  Religious Studies
University of Scranton

Peter L. Berger
University Professors Program
Boston University

James H. Billington
Woodrow Wilson International
  Center for Scholars

Allan Carlson
The Rockford Institute

Jean Bethke Elshtain
Department of Political Science
University of Massachusetts

Joel L. Fleishman
Duke University

Charles Glenn
Department of Education
The Commonwealth of
Massachusetts

Stanley Hauerwas
The Divinity School
Duke University

James Hitchcock
Department of History
St. Louis University

Everett Carll Ladd
The Roper Center
University of Connecticut

C. Eric Lincoln
Department of Religion
Duke University

Rockne McCarthy
Studies Institute
Dordt College

Gilbert Meilaender
Department of Religion
Oberlin College

Richard John Neuhaus
The Rockford Institute Center
  on Religion & Society

Michael Novak
American Enterprise Institute
  for Public Policy Research

James Nuechterlein
The Cresset
Valparaiso University

Robert Payton
Exxon Education Foundation

Robert E. Rodes, Jr.
School of Law
Notre Dame University

Bernard Semmel
Department of History
State University of New York
  at Stony Brook

Paul T. Stallsworth
The Rockford Institute Center
  on Religion & Society

Margaret Steinfels
National Pastoral Life Center

tion rules, though, we must take another step. The aim of measures dealing with these subjects is not to elicit specific good acts or discourage specific bad ones. It is, as I just said, to enhance social amenities and see to their just distribution. To relate this aim to the pursuit of virtue, I turn to *Gaudium et Spes*, the Second Vatican Council's Pastoral Constitution on the Church in the Modern World. Unlike earlier philosophical and theological teachings, this document links social amenities closely with human fulfillment:

> Man's social nature makes it evident that the progress of the human person and the advance of society itself hinge on each other. For the beginning, the subject, and the goal of all social institutions is and must be the human person, which for its part and by its very nature stands completely in need of social life. This social life is not something added on to man. Hence, through his dealings with others, through reciprocal duties, and through fraternal dialogue he develops all his gifts and is able to rise to his destiny.

That destiny is to be perfected in virtue. It follows, then, that virtue is the end of social life, and what I have called social amenities are society's contribution to virtue. The law's function of enhancing and distributing these amenities, therefore, is referable to its function of leading people to virtue.

Earlier sources have tended to obscure this doctrine by distinguishing too sharply between earthly and heavenly kingdoms or between our temporal and spiritual ends. However, St. Thomas moves in the direction of the doctrine when he says that if a law is properly ordered to the common good, it will tend to make people good absolutely, whereas if it is ordered to something inappropriate, it will make people good only in a narrow sense—in the sense that a man might be said to be a good robber if he knows how to rob efficiently. *Gaudium et Spes* relates this claim of St. Thomas about the common good to the claim that the law is meant to enhance social amenities by defining the common good as "the sum total of social conditions which allow people, either as groups or as individuals, to reach their fulfillment more fully and more easily."

Insofar as the enhancement and distribution of social amenities can be referred to the pursuit of virtue, so can the salvage function of law. When the law intervenes in a tragic situation, it does so to restore the social support the victims need to survive and grow—the dealings with others, reciprocal duties, and fraternal dialogue mentioned in *Gaudium et Spes*.

I believe these reflections on *Gaudium et Spes* indicate that the tenets of sociological jurisprudence can be reconciled with the claim that law should lead people to virtue. The significance of such a reconciliation depends of course on how we value sociological jurisprudence. It is a doctrine that comes out of modern technology—witness Roscoe Pound's famous metaphor of "social engineering"—and has both the strengths and the weaknesses of that technology. It offers the law a more sophisticated set of incentives and disincentives to work with than it had under the traditional notion of orders backed by threats, but it is still limited to the production of desirable behavior by manipulation of those incentives and disincentives. If law is something more than a technology for eliciting desirable patterns of behavior, then sociological jurisprudence is something less than an adequate account of it.

The technological approach has had its technological successes. It has served to enhance at crucial points the "social conditions which allow people . . . to reach their fulfillment more fully and more easily." It has put an end to a number of useless and pernicious legal dispositions from the rotten borough to the destructibility of contingent remainders. It has supported legislation abolishing the yellow-dog contract and the twelve-hour workday. It has freed the urban slum dweller from the feudal principles that made it possible for a landlord to collect rent without fixing the toilet. Its stern critique has brought about a total remodeling of civil procedure. In many ways, in short, it has served us well.

But the unrelieved pragmatism of the approach becomes destructive at the very point where the social conditions for virtue are to be translated into virtue itself. It subjects the whole legal enterprise to a rigorous bottom-line critique that it is not well able to withstand. If law is a mere instrument, it is not all that good a one. Inevitably, our ability to perceive defects and inefficiencies is more widespread and more far-reaching than our ability to cope with them. Inevitably, criticisms pile up more rapidly than reforms. From being seen as a way of getting things done, the law comes to be seen as a way of not getting things done, or as a way of getting them done badly. If people see law as nothing more than a useful tool, they will come to see it as a failure, and eventually as an enemy. They will not be able to find in it an adequate matrix for their responsibilities to one another. They will not be able to feel the moral force of society behind its dispositions or to perceive that being a good neighbor or a good citizen has anything to do with living by it.

I believe, therefore, that we cannot be content with leaving the pursuit of virtue to the bottom-line legal theories that define law by its deployment of incentives and disincentives and evaluate it in terms of its social effects. These matters are important, but they are not ultimate criteria. They must be looked at from within the context of what I call a *jurisprudence of aspirations,* by which I mean a treatment of law as an expression of what we aspire to as a community—which is not necessarily what we can realistically hope to accomplish.

If as a community we aspire to live virtuously, to deal virtuously with one another, to encourage and support one another in leading virtuous lives, then the law must bear an effective witness to the whole of that aspiration rather than merely coerce or manipulate a measure of compliance with some part. It was no sentimentalist or visionary, but the ever-practical Justice Holmes who said that "The law is the witness and external deposit of our moral life. Its history is the history of the moral development of the race. The practice of it, in spite of popular jests, tends to make good citizens and good men." If we concern ourselves only with what can or should be enforced, we overlook this function of our law, and, as a consequence, badly attenuate the moral life of our society.

Wherever there is moral concern in a social context, the law has an important role to play whether or not it can be effectively enforced. It confronts the individual conscience with the community's judgment about what is acceptable and what is to be encouraged. It offers the fruit of detached and informed moral reflection to people who have to act suddenly and under pressure. It represents the community's choice among different ways of implementing a general moral principle. As the scholastic philosophers put it, positive law makes specific what natural law (i.e., morality) leaves general.

It is through this kind of moral positioning that the law exercises much of its power to promote virtue and to support, vindicate, or protect the social conditions in which virtue can be sought. The law's massive witness against the criminal does as much to deter crime as does the fear of punishment. Poor people, if they are to live virtuously, need the community concern expressed in the welfare laws almost as much as they need the money. These are two areas in which the pragmatic approach has proved especially destructive—offering fear without moral suasion in the one case and money without compassion or respect in the other.

The task of moral positioning is complicated but not superseded by the complementary pragmatic task of deploying incentives to virtuous conduct or disincentives to the opposite. The moral positioning is often needed in circumstances where incentives and disincentives cannot be effectively deployed, and sometimes in circumstances where they cannot be justly deployed. It is especially needed in circumstances where they are being deployed in the wrong way.

Moral positioning evokes a good deal of controversy that purports to be about something else. The question of the legal status of consensual sex is often put in pragmatic terms—Is the time of the police and the prosecutor well spent in prosecuting victimless crimes?—but the real dynamic is provided by the hidden agenda of giving or not giving moral validity to the conduct in question. For my own part, I would like to see this conduct neither persecuted nor validated; I would therefore favor keeping the old laws on the books and giving them the sparse enforcement they have always had.

But it is not only in the realm of sex that there are moral principles that should not be enforced with the full power of the state but that a legal system worthy of a decent society cannot ignore. Our antitrust laws, our multiple-dwelling laws, our stock promotion laws, and especially our civil rights laws all have dispositions whose reach exceeds their grasp. Nevertheless, without them our body of law would be severely impaired in stature, and far less capable of promoting a virtuous life.

The jurisprudence of aspirations puts the relation between law and virtue on a very different footing than does the juridical triumphalism of the New Right. I have read of a judge who refuses to recite the Pledge of Allegiance to the flag on the grounds that it is not true that this nation offers "liberty and justice for all." I believe the New Right (or the Old Right for that matter) would respond, "Well maybe not *all*, but *nearly* all—if you liberals don't spoil it." Taking a strictly empirical view of the matter, I am with the judge. This is not and never has been a nation with liberty and justice for all or nearly all, and probably not even for a bare majority. But I do not take an empirical view. What makes our country special is not what it is or what it has been, but what we and generations of our predecessors have wanted and still want it to be. It is in that spirit that I recite the Pledge of Allegiance, and in the same spirit that I examine the relation between law and virtue.

As statements of what we aspire to, our laws give us no basis for congratulating ourselves. As much as they bear witness to our desire to live virtuously together, they also bear witness to how far we have fallen short of doing so. Even such technically successful measures as, say, the Fourteenth Amendment or the National Labor Relations Act are more a product of our common suffering than an excuse for complacency. Laws like these are made for use, and we often use them to good effect, but it is not their effectiveness that gives them their power to lead people to virtue. They are aspirations written in the blood of our people—at Cold Harbor and Shiloh, in Watts and Selma, in the Chicago Haymarket and in Harlan County, Kentucky. Whether we or our ancestors played a noble or an ignoble part in these confrontations, they encourage us to approach the common pursuit of virtue with a good deal of humility.

A jurisprudence of aspirations will not only prevent the development of some destructive elements in the law but will also give people a way of coping with the destructive elements that inevitably do arise. Even without accepting the traditional theory that an unjust law is no law at all, we can see the unjust use of legal forms or legal apparatus as a wound or a violence inflicted on the law. Brutal policemen, inept and uncaring bureaucrats, venal legislators, and corrupt judges make of the law not an accomplice but a victim.

Bottom-line theorists will hold that it is not acceptable to view the law as a source of moral positioning and, a fortiori, as a victim because they feel that to do so tends to bring the whole legal system into disrepute. They argue that people will lose respect for the law if they see it intruding into situations where it cannot deliver a technically effective result. This would be a serious objection if the facts bore it out. But they do not. We have whole generations of peasants, laborers, students, welfare recipients, peace demonstrators, and social activists to tell us that it is power, not the lack of it, that causes people to lose respect for the law.

The *locus classicus* on this question is international law. The bottom-line critics tend to say that this body of material is not really law at all because no one enforces it, and, indeed, when a hard case rises, almost no one obeys it. The bottom-line objection is as persuasive here as it will ever be: we can argue about how much we accomplish with laws against marijuana or bucket shops, but only in the international realm can it be seriously contended that law accomplishes nothing at all. If law does in fact accomplish something in the international realm, where there is neither administration nor enforcement, it must accomplish that and more in other realms where there is even a modicum of both.

In fact, international law accomplishes a great deal—simply by the moral positioning it affords. There are matters such as seal hunting or the transmission of mail where it is followed by almost everyone almost all the time. In matters such as the exploitation of the ocean floor, governments are negotiating to set up new rules—evidently with the intention of following them once they are set up. Even in the heat of battle, combatants often follow the rules of international law, accepting some military disadvantage to do so. And where the level of compliance is not all that we might wish, international law nonetheless provides the language of moral discourse concerning matters to which it applies. People claim to be following it even when they are not, and they use it to justify their positions as best they can. Both corporations and governments pay lawyers well to master its principles and use them in argument.

Respect for international law seems in no way to be diminished by the impunity—indeed, the insouciance—with which it is violated. Its vulnerability, its inability to back its moral suasion with any kind of power, seems almost universally to be regarded as cause for regret, not scorn. Compared with other kinds of law, it loses nothing in public esteem from the fact that the uniformed men who go around spreading terror are generally violating it, not enforcing it.

My effort so far has been to restate and support the traditional doctrine that law is meant to lead people to virtue in the light of the modern perception that it is meant to do other things—support liberty, enhance and distribute social amenities, and help pick up the pieces when things go wrong. I have saved for last the most cogent objection to my doctrine—namely, the problem of who, in a pluralist society, is to decide what constitutes virtue. Who is entitled to embody the notions of virtue in the law under which we all will have to live? This is not a matter of freedom; I have already recognized that issue and accepted an obligation to respect it. Rather, the objection consists of the claim that the law must be strictly neutral regarding one version of virtue and another. It is not a claim that people outside the mainstream must be respected; it is a claim that there is no mainstream. It is not a claim for the rights of dissenters; it is a claim that there is nothing to dissent from.

Before looking at this claim philosophically, we should note that its consequences are pernicious. First, it deprives us of any basis for imposing accountability on the people who are running our country. It radically privatizes all values. And without public values, we have no way of challenging what business people, administrators, doctors, soldiers, and (alas!) lawyers are doing with their professional skills.

The claim is also pernicious in that it exposes people to harmful social influences that the law has no way of countering. It is possible for the law to be neutral regarding different notions of virtue, but it is hardly possible for a whole society to be. People make decisions about how they will live in the midst of a welter of conflicting social influences. The question is whether and to what extent one of those influences will be the law. If we try to remove the law from this catalogue of influences, there will be no lack of candidates for the vacancy it leaves—and a good many will be more dangerous than the law.

The philosophical grounding for this baneful privatization of values seems to be jointly attributable to Descartes and Hume. Mainstream Western philosophy took from Descartes the view that beyond sense data nothing can be affirmed with certainty except logical deductions from self-evident principles, and from Hume it received the view that value judgments cannot be derived from sense data. From these premises, it has generally been concluded that value judgments are matters of mere personal preference on the order of liking or not liking parsnips. A corollary is that the law has no more reason to be concerned with values than with whether or not people eat parsnips. For two centuries political and legal philosophers have been trying to avoid this conclusion or mitigate its destructive consequences without abandoning the premises on which it is based. They have not succeeded.

I believe we should meet these premises head on. To do so, I would appeal to natural law. There are of course a number of different accounts of this concept on the market, but there is no need to choose one here. To overcome the privatization of values we need only recognize that we can employ connatural judgments about values (i.e., judgments arrived at through experiencing the human condition as a participant) in evaluating and shaping the law. To accept natural law is to accept that such judgments are a source of knowledge and that systematic reflection on them can yield philosophical truth.

In mainstream Catholic theology, and in those Protestant traditions that accept natural law, it is assumed that revelation guides and supports our capacity for making connatural judgments without in any way superseding it. With this approach, it is possible to maintain philosophical and theological judgments in considerable harmony, and, indeed, to maintain them without being too concerned about which is which.

Connatural judgments may legitimately be proposed as sources of values in a pluralist society because, whether they are couched in philosophical or theological terms, they are communicated on the basis of shared experiences of the human condition. They will not have consequences for the law unless they come to command something like a consensus. In fact, I think there is in our society a broader connatural consensus than we sometimes suppose. It is the philosophical privatization of values that has led us to discount that consensus and look for some other basis for our laws.

Natural law doctrine, then, with its appeal to connatural judgments as a source of value and philosophical truth, meets the prevailing philosophy on the subject head on. Advocates of the prevailing philosophy respond to this challenge with both theoretical and practical attacks on natural law doctrine.

The theoretical objection is basically circular. It is claimed that the proposition that judgments constitute a source of truth different from either logical deduction or empirical observation cannot be accepted because it is neither a logical deduction nor an empirical observation. This argument deserves much shorter shrift than it generally gets.

The practical objection is that natural law doctrine is at

once anarchic and despotic. Since the judgments to which it appeals are neither logically deducible nor empirically observable, it is impossible to get people to agree on them. If one person may legitimately impose his or her version on other people, every other person may legitimately do the same. The resulting chaos will not end until one of the contenders overcomes the others by brute force.

Experience entirely fails to bear this objection out. Certainly there have been serious and destructive disagreements about the content of natural law, but there have been equally serious and destructive disagreements about what legal principles can be logically or empirically arrived at. On the whole, shared experience of being human and shared intuitions of how human beings ought to live have commanded a broader consensus in society than any but the most rudimentary of logical deductions or empirical observations.

Nor does history support the popular view that connatural judgments have tended to support bad institutions while logical or empirical judgments have supported good ones. For instance, the nineteenth-century arguments in favor of slavery in this country were on the whole empirical, while the arguments against it were on the whole connatural. Similarly, the excesses of industrial capitalism were on the whole supported by logical or empirical reasoning and resisted on connatural grounds. The cold logic of utilitarianism was rigorously invoked in favor of laissez-faire economics, while Marx's and Engel's critiques, although they purport to be scientific, in fact bristle with connatural outrage.

In our own century, the death camp personnel and the designers and builders of gas ovens relied on the logic of obedience to superiors and the attainment of abstract goals to overcome their connatural aversion to what they were given to do. It is well known that the German legal community responded to the Nazi experience by turning almost en masse to natural law doctrine after World War II.

The key concepts for a natural law approach to the institutions of a free pluralist society are dialogue and respect. Because natural law is based on the validity of connatural judgments, and connatural judgments are communicated through shared experience, it is always possible for people to talk about points on which they differ in the light of what they have in common. At the same time, by sharing the experience of being human, they share the experience of being unique. Every person can recognize every other person as having a particular version of the common destiny to work out, the common predicament to undergo. Every person is like every other person in having his or her own ways of doing so. In this context, pluralism and the promotion of virtue go hand in hand. Just as everyone needs incentives to be good, and everyone needs guidance, so everyone needs space.

As for the question of who is to decide what constitutes virtue, the answer is that we all are. We must remember that law is primarily not a thing done but a thing said. If police officers or judges set out to make it effective, it is because they have read or heard that that is what they are supposed to do. Before we address laws and proposed laws to these officials, we address them to one another. They are the language of moral discourse in our society. Through them we offer guidance, motivation, encouragement, and space to one another and claim or accept the same at each other's hands. The process is always subtle, sometimes shrill, and never neat. But on the whole, if allowed to operate, it produces what it is meant to produce—a legally supported consensus about how we may live virtuously together without either suppressing our differences or privatizing our values. We may suppose that such a consensus, if allowed to develop freely over a long time (as it has never been), would grow closer and closer to a traditional Christian understanding of virtue. "For," we read in *Gaudium et Spes*, "the Church knows full well that her message is in harmony with the most secret desires of the human heart."

Democracy, Virtue, and Religion: A Historical Perspective

Bernard Semmel

This essay presents a view of the relationship between democracy and virtue from the standpoint of history rather than from the more familiar perspective of political philosophy. Since I deal primarily with the United States and England in the past three centuries, the role of religion is a central issue. Any effort to discuss so complex a problem in a short essay must be somewhat idiosyncratic. In this case, what may seem a surprising yoking of the doctrines of evangelical Arminianism and the perception of a democratic virtue by the leading nineteenth-century rationalist philosopher is the outcome of two studies I have made which deal with these subjects.* I discuss the difficulties confronting a regime of virtue in a pluralist democracy supported by different and at times conflicting moral bases in these volumes; in this essay it is as much as I can do merely to allude to these difficulties. A secularist might question whether believers can accept any basis for a moral life other than their own; many believers would ask the same question and proceed to argue that the idea of a freely chosen—as opposed to divinely sanctioned—virtue is specious, and the acceptance of different bases of virtue is at best patronizing.

---

* *The Methodist Revolution* (New York: Basic Books, 1973) and *John Stuart Mill and the Pursuit of Virtue* (New Haven: Yale University Press, 1984).

The traditional view of democracy from Aristotle through the nineteenth century was that the passions and interests of the ruling majority would imperil the survival of virtue and of liberty, with which virtue was often linked. The history of the ancient Greek city states and of Rome was cited as evidence. Political philosophers contended that virtue (understood as obedience to a moral standard and a preference for the public over the private good) and the liberty to assume control of one's life so as to direct it toward moral goals were more likely to flourish in an aristocratic or even a monarchical state. When such states turned to popular government, factious politics stifled liberty and undermined civic morals; soon these states could no longer manage their internal affairs or defend themselves against external enemies. They fell victim to oligarchs and despots or to foreign domination.

*   *   *

When it became clear by the end of the eighteenth century that some form of democratic government would prevail in the modern Western state, political theorists speculated about how they might avoid the fate of the ancient democracies. Montesquieu, in the spirit of the Enlightenment, described constitutional forms that would protect liberty and civic virtue, and the authors of the American Constitution devised a system of checks and balances that they hoped would prevent the interests of factions and the passions of masses from subverting the public good. However useful such a system, a number of political theorists suggested that even the best constitutional mechanisms would by themselves be inadequate. Rousseau advocated a civil religion to preserve a good society, but such a solution proved to have serious defect. In the 1770s Rousseau's disciple Robespierre executed a plan to impose a republic of virtue in which individual freedom had no place; this culminated in the worship of the goddess Liberty and the bloody fanaticism of the Reign of Terror. In the 1850s Auguste Comte proposed a religion of humanity—also designed to impose a regime of virtue—that embodied a civil religion not only hostile to individual happiness and destructive of liberty but ridiculous to all but a small group of intellectuals.

A contemporary of Comte, the liberal democrat John Stuart Mill, rejected the French positivist's vision of an imposed virtue